Relief from Candida

ALLERGIES AND ILL HEALTH

D0279134

Greta Sichel ND DO and Michael Sichel ND DO

Foreword by Dr Joachim Fluhrer MB BS

Introduction by Dr Richard Mackarness MB BS DPM
(Author of *Not All In The Mind, Chemical Victims*
and *A Little of What You Fancy*)

SALLY MILNER PUBLISHING

First published in 1990 by
Sally Milner Publishing Pty Ltd
558 Darling Street
Rozelle NSW 2039 Australia

Reprinted 1991, 1993, 1995

© Sichel, Greta. 1990

Illustrations by Daphne Gooley
Photography by Andre Martin
Typeset in 11/13 pt Garamond by
Trade Graphics Pty Ltd, Melbourne
Printed in Australia by
Australian Print Group

National Library of Australia
Cataloguing-in-Publication data:

Sichel, Greta..
   Relief from Candida, allergies and ill health.

   Includes index.
   ISBN 1 86351 001 X

   1.Candidiasis — Diet therapy. 2. Allergy —
   Diet therapy. 3. Candidiasis — Diet therapy —
   Recipes. 4. Allergy — Diet therapy — Recipes.
   5. Diet therapy. I. Title.

616.969

Front cover:
The Golden Age (detail)
Aby Altson c. 1867 — c. 1949 Australian
oil on canvas, 248.9 x 137.8 cm
Purchased with the assistance of a scholarship, 1895
National Gallery of Victoria

CONTENTS

NOT JUST ANOTHER COOKBOOK

A foreword by Dr Joachim Fluhrer

The last decade has been one of amazing advances in well-documented scientific research concerning nutrition and its effects in health and disease.

Relief from Candida is based on the practical application of this knowledge gained by years of experience in helping people to get well and stay well by the co-authors Greta and Michael Sichel.

Nutrition is an ongoing science that I find fundamental in my practice of environmental medicine. This practical book should be invaluable for the thousands of 'victims of the twentieth century' whose food sensitivities and often accompanying candida overgrowth need a special approach in the kitchen. I find that many of my patients need practical instruction in obtaining the correct foods and preparing them. The many and varied recipes and weekly programme will give me an invaluable educational guide to recommend to my patients.

Dr Joachim Fluhrer MB BS
Nutritional Medicine

PREFACE

The need for this cookbook became apparent to me and my husband over the last few years that we operated our live-in clinic, Fountaindale Clinic, at Ourimbah, north of Gosford.

My husband Dr Michael Sichel ND, DO went over to Mexico to accompany a very seriously ill candida patient to a biological clinic there, operated by American Biologics. He came back an expert on the candida problem and acquired equipment to diagnose this and other conditions.

As a result we detected that we had many patients suffering from candida albicans overload and also allergies. As I was in charge of nutrition it was my unenviable task to find suitable recipes for these patients, all with differing allergies. It was a task that required a lot of imagination.

The result is this cookbook with recipes that are suitable for basic candida sufferers. Because of the vast number of potential allergies people may suffer from, it cannot cater for every possible allergy non-related to candida. You may have to replace or leave out some of the substances according to your individual requirements, e.g. substitute one type of grain or flour for another.

If you have been treated for candida and follow-up allergy tests are positive, it is possible to challenge the allergic food items one by one and overcome the allergic reactions. None of the allergens should be eaten more often than once every four days, better still once a week.

To assist you with this we have included at least fourteen of each type of dish, except fish and staple dishes, of which there are at least seven. After using this book for a while you will learn to use other recipes by substituting some of the ingredients for the non-allergy ones.

The product information list will give you an idea of the not-so-familiar items you can buy. If not obtainable in supermarkets, they are sold in health food stores or delicatessens.

Because of the prevalence of hypoglycaemia in candida patients we strongly recommend making an effort to switch over to our easy to follow daily eating programme.

The candida diet was written by my husband for his patients. I am also indebted to him for urging me to compile this cookbook.

I would like to acknowledge my secretary, Janine Christensen, who not only typed the manuscript, but offered many valuable suggestions.

I also acknowledge Jenny Kingsland BA VA (Hons) Newcastle University for the sketched illustrations and Stephen McDonald, qualified cook specialising in health foods, for perfecting the cake recipe.

Greta Sichel ND, DO

WHAT IS CANDIDA?

An introduction by Dr Richard Mackarness

Not so long ago, few doctors would put candidiasis (candida albicans) high on the list of possible diagnoses when confronted with a patient complaining of multiple symptoms. Today this is no longer true. Candida must be considered in every case where the diagnosis is not immediately apparent.

What has caused this change? What used to be seen as a not-too-serious, localised infection has become something much more generalised, affecting not only the traditional thrush areas (mouth and vagina) but mucous membranes throughout the gut and respiratory passages. The toxins produced by candida in these areas act on every part of the body, including the nervous system.

To understand why this change has taken place it is necessary to look at the natural history of candida albicans and the changes which have occurred in its human alimentary environment or, in other words, the changes in the diet which candida shares with its human hosts.

Candida albicans is a type of microscopic yeast in a sub-group of fungi or moulds. Moulds are everywhere. They occur in soil, on plants, in the air and in and on all living creatures. We all have candida organisms on our skin and on the mucous membranes lining all body cavities. Normally, the presence of candida should cause no problems. As with bacteria and other micro-organisms, a balance is struck between factors favouring and inhibiting proliferation.

Lately, however, several things have happened to disturb this balance in favour of candida overgrowth. The most

11

important of these is the change in our diet from the traditional meat and two veg, low in refined carbohydrate, to fast foods rich in sugars and other simple carbohydrates on which candida feeds. Add to this the widespread prescription of antibiotics which kill off bacteria that compete with candida, plus birth control pills and cortisone-type drugs that depress our immune systems, and we have a potentially disastrous effect on the fragile internal ecosystem in which candida has hitherto been kept in check.

More and more people are now showing symptoms attributable to candida overgrowth, from flare-up of vulvo-vaginitis with itching and discharge and the white-coated tongue of oral thrush, to heartburn, abdominal pain, diarrhoea, constipation, coughs, sore throats, itchy rashes, muscle and joint pains, depression, anxiety, irritability, headaches and confusion. Most of these diverse symptoms are the result of allergic reactions to toxic metabolites released when candida organisms die.

The solution to this problem is not simple. An anti-yeast type antibiotic will help in the short term, but for lasting results a more radical approach is required. This means changing the environment in which candida thrives, resting the immune system and stimulating resistance, which can be achieved in the following ways:

- Adopt a diet designed to starve candida out. This is by far the most important single measure and is the subject of this book.
- Take regular vitamin and mineral supplements to boost the immune system.
- Avoid anti-bacterial broad-spectrum antibiotics and steroids (birth-control pills and cortisone-type hormones).
- Avoid yeast spores within the atmosphere in the home by cleaning up and drying out damp and mouldy areas in bathrooms, under sinks etc.
- Ask your doctor for a course of graded injections of candida extract, to create specific immunity against this yeast.

This excellent book tells you exactly what foods to avoid and what to eat instead. From the wide range of foods allowed, recipes are given to suit all tastes and to help avoid foods to which some people may be allergic, quite apart from any candida problem.

To finish, a note about food allergies. Many people know from past experience that certain foods do not agree with them and in some cases actually make them ill. This can complicate candidiasis, which, by damaging the lining of the gut, facilitates the absorption of food allergens that an intact gut might keep out. There are now doctors in all major cities who specialise in food allergies. There may be one attached to the allergy clinic of your local hospital. Your GP can give you a referral.

Dr Richard Mackarness
Author of *Not All in the Mind* and *Chemical Victims*.

THE BACKGROUND STORY

Candida — Potent Cause of Allergies

Candida albicans, the yeast-like fungus involved in 'thrush', or 'monilia', cannot be considered in isolation, as it also lies behind many other symptoms, including allergies. To understand the problems associated with candida, therefore, it is important to have an understanding of allergies.

You will notice that the recipes in this book do not contain sugar in any form (except an occasional green apple). This is because candida fungus lives on sugars of all kinds — even fruit sugars or honey.

But other foods you should avoid if you have this problem — such as Vegemite, soya sauce and fermented beverages, etc — do not actually feed candida organisms. The reason they should be avoided is that they contain yeasts and those who suffer from candida will certainly be allergic to them.

The ABC of Allergies

In early 1989 The *Australian* newspaper published an account of the King family, Howard and Marilyn and their two children, who live in a tin shed by the sea on Kangaroo Island off South Australia.

Ex-Queenslanders who had been exposed to herbicides thirteen years before, the Kings became victims of the worst form of allergy — Total Allergy.

As its name implies, Total Allergy Syndrome leaves its victims with a sensitivity to almost any substance with a volatile chemical nature — from lipstick to wildflowers, from plastics

15

in any form to a wide variety of foods, and from petrol fumes and paints to even the ink with which this page is printed.

The *Australian* article exposed the tip of the iceberg. It is now agreed among most environmental doctors that sixty per cent of the population is sensitive to some degree to the twentieth century.

In the USA the public body that monitors disease, the Centre for Disease Control, recently announced that 1.2 million Americans currently suffer from Universal Reaction (the name given for Total Allergy Syndrome in the USA). This term is used to define allergy sufferers who are unable to work an eight-hour day. This of course does not take account of the many millions suffering from less devastating allergy loads.

These sensitivities lie behind many unexplained health problems in the community. Often these problems include extreme fatigue, depression, nausea, bloating, itching and dazed or spaced-out feelings. Too often they are diagnosed as being so-called 'virus induced' illnesses.

Sensitising Chemicals

Total Allergy Syndrome, as experienced by the King family, is often caused by an initial exposure to what are called 'sensitising' chemicals. These chemicals alter the body's immune system so that the victim, who once had a normal resistance to chemical pollutants and natural chemicals in his environment, suddenly finds himself/herself reeling under the impact of strange and unwelcome symptoms.

One common, and dangerous, sensitising chemical is formaldehyde. Formaldehyde is a chemical used far too commonly in our homes. It is in the glues that bind our chipboard floors, cupboards and furniture, and in the foams that make our lounge-room chairs. Wallpaper, wallboards, paints, building glues and adhesives, plus some beverages (wine and beer) and some cosmetics all contain formaldehyde.

Formaldehyde not only sensitises us (making our immune

system prone to chemicals that would not normally bother us) but has recently been proven to be a mutagenic agent. A mutagen causes cells to change in nature and is a precursor to cancer. Formaldehyde's carcinogenic property was initially found on experiments with rats, who developed nasal cancer, but human cancer has now also been shown to develop from formaldehyde exposure.

Food Allergies

Another, and much more common, form of allergy is food sensitivity. It is primarily for those suffering from this form of allergy that this book has been written. (Although those suffering from any type of allergic reactivity will benefit from a low food allergy diet.)

For many years we operated our own naturopathic 'hospital' or live-in clinic (Fountaindale, in New South Wales) and it was there that we began to become aware how serious and widespread is the problem of food sensitivity.

It is important to look seriously at the possibility that a patient is suffering from food allergies before resorting to medical drugs, which, we find, can often compound the problems lying behind so much unexplained illness. One five and a half year old boy was brought to me because of a serious and chronic sneezing problem. He had been sneezing on and off for five years, sometimes sneezing a hundred times without stopping, and his mother had been unable to find help anywhere.

By examining his diet, which contained the usual sort of monotonous foods upon which the average Australian child is raised, and asking a few pertinent questions about the boy's bowel habits and whether he had wind or a bloated stomach, it was possible to detect the problem. The boy had an allergy to milk, wheat and oranges. With a change in the boy's eating habits and the aid of some digestive enzyme tablets, the boy's sneezing problem was soon a thing of the past.

It is not always as easy as this to determine the foods to

which a person is allergic. Two methods used by us in our clinic are the Pulse Test and Cytotoxic Testing (the laboratory testing of a blood sample for metabolic intolerance, which is about seventy per cent accurate). In the pulse test, one takes the basal pulse, the lowest pulse of the day, for one minute on waking. The pulse rate is recorded, as is the resting pulse before each meal, and it is again recorded at three half-hourly intervals after each meal. Normally the pulse rate should not vary more than about eighteen beats per minute. Any variations over this are evidence of some allergy reaction to one or more of the foods eaten at the previous meal.

One hyperactive thirteen year old who came to us because of his violent and aggressive behaviour was diagnosed as having thirty-six allergic reactions out of a possible seventy. Several of these were severe and almost all of them related to foods which he commonly ate. This is typical of many allergy victims, who are frequently allergic to the foods that they eat most often and in the greatest quantity.

This is why the most common food allergies vary from country to country. In the USA, for instance, you will easily see why their top ten food allergies are (in order): milk (and all dairy products); chocolate and cola; corn; eggs; peanuts; citrus fruits; tomato; wheat; cinnamon and food colourings.

Australians will probably guess what some of the top ten allergens are in this country too. Here they are in order: milk; fruits; corn; eggs; rye; yeast; peanuts; prawns and seafoods; malt; barley. Potatoes are also high on the list (thirty-seven per cent of people tested from one clinic were allergic to potatoes. But these were all people with health problems).

Other common allergenic foods include: wheat; chocolate; oranges; tobacco; coffee; tea; pork; oysters; curry; apples; strawberries; many culinary herbs and spices and many food additives.

Biological Individuality

You may ask, 'Why doesn't every person react to foods like these ones?'

One answer lies in our incredible individuality. Just as each of us has a unique fingerprint, personality and physical features, so we all have a unique biochemistry. Not only do we have a different external appearance to anybody else, we are different on the inside!

Unfortunately biochemical weaknesses can be passed on in the same way as any other hereditary defect. This is why the clinics of environmental doctors often have several generations from the same family visiting them.

About fifteen per cent of allergies are linked with an inborn faulty metabolism. Every week I see two or three mothers who consult me about their own allergy problems and then say to me, at the end of the consultation: 'I must bring my son/daughter — they have just the same problems as I have!'

Genetics, Allergies and Cancer

The definite link between hereditary disposition to certain immune deficiency diseases, including cancer, and food sensitivities is recorded in a fascinating book by the well-known Sydney doctor, Chris Reading. Called *Relatively Speaking* (Fontana/Collins, Sydney, 1984) the book describes some quite amazing case histories of the complete reversal of advanced cancer by eliminating certain foods from the patient's diet.

This is why a low allergy diet is also likely to be a low cancer diet. In 1982 the US National Academy of Sciences prepared a report on Diet, Nutrition and Cancer. The report showed that thirty to forty per cent of cancers in men and sixty per cent of cancers in women are due to diet.

It is likely that the situation is similar here, given the relative similarities in our diets. The major culprits are: fats; smoked or salt-cured foods; low fibre foods; and food additives and chemicals.

Not long ago I consulted with a Total Allergy type lady who was typical of the cases described in the book *Relatively Speaking*. Her mother and three out of four of her aunts had allergies and had later developed cancer.

For fifteen years she had come to grips with her own allergies and had made a chart that showed her predictable reactions to many foods. Her hard work had paid off and she was able to keep herself and her children (who were also food sensitive) in a good state of health.

The Mechanism of Allergies

Food sensitivity results when 'foreign' proteins or particles find their way into the bloodstream. The mechanism is not yet fully understood. However, the body's team of 'immigration officers' — the immune system specialist blood cells, will not allow strangers into your body without a passport. The 'passport' is in the form of a set of your own genes that are attached to virtually every cell in your body. These molecules, attached to the surface of your cells, positively identify them as natural residents. But foreign visitors have other molecules (called antigens) attached to their surface. Immediately these antigens are detected the police anti-body squad is summonsed, and various mechanisms begin to operate.

One of these is the release of histamines from special cells called mast cells. This causes the production of much fluid and is the reason for the familiar sneezing and watery eyes and nose associated with allergies. The fluid retention of allergy oedema is designed to limit the damage done by the foreign proteins. It is also the cause of much of the bloated, overweight problems experienced by allergic women. Many women consult us and say, 'But I hardly eat anything, and yet cannot lose weight. In fact, sometimes, the less I eat the more I seem to put on weight'.

By positively identifying the foods to which these poor women are allergic, we find they soon improve.

Another important cause of food sensitivity is a so-called 'leaky bowel'. Dr John Hunter, a researcher at Addenbrooke's Hospital in Cambridge (UK), has observed that the use of large dose antibiotics causes a depletion of natural bowel flora (friendly bacteria). These protective bacteria play what is seen to be an increasingly important role in keeping our bowel wall (mucous membrane) healthy and efficient. Any major depletion allows substances to pass too easily into the bloodstream.

Dr Hunter's observations were made during a double-blind controlled trial with hysterectomy patients receiving pre-op antibiotic prevention programmes.

Overgrowth of candida albicans (a normal but usually controlled inhabitant of the healthy bowel) is encouraged by antibiotics and also by a fermentative sugary diet. On becoming active it changes into a thread-like (mycelial) form that can invade the mucous membrane of the bowel and cause increased permeability.

In fact there are several mechanisms that can cause food sensitivity. Most researchers believe that a combination of these factors probably account for most of the problems.

One interesting protective mechanism that can sometimes fail us because of abuse is the Peyer Patch programme. Peyer's Patches are small groups of lymphatic cells in the intestine. These cells constantly absorb fluid from the passing stream of the intestine and 'label' the various foods with an 'OK signal' that makes sure the 'policemen' further down the gut don't make a mistaken 'arrest' — which causes an inflammatory reaction.

For the scientifically minded — the 'OK' mark is made by immunoglobulin SIgA. This signal activates B cells in readiness to produce more 'OK' markers wherever the antigen may appear. These activated B cells bear only the one signal, or antibody 'OK', and multiply to inhabit even the most distant of the body's mucous membrane surfaces.

If the food molecule (antigen) does enter the blood, then 'T' cells recognise the antigen and keep the response 'normal' by suppressing and/or helping the B cells which produce the regulatory SIgA immunoglobulin.

If for some reason this identifying mechanism fails, then reactions, ranging from mild to life-threatening in effect, can occur. We have seen several people, for instance, who have been hospitalised after eating tropical edible fish. Their throats swelled with their reaction, causing near-asphyxiation.

This type of reaction is a true allergy. It is somewhat different to a food intolerance, which is not so dramatic and is sometimes masked or hard to identify as a cause of health problems, but over a period can nevertheless cause a major breakdown of health.

We are often asked, 'Will I always be allergic to these foods?'

The answer is not always the same. Some foods can be tolerated by eating them less frequently (called rotation); the rotation periods will vary from food to food and with different people. Most rotation periods range from four to ten days apart.

This allows the body to dispose of the offending food proteins. Other foods can later become tolerated by improving the digestive processes. Poor digestion, usually through a lack of stomach acid and pancreas and liver enzymes, fails to break down the food properly, resulting in larger than normal food components (peptides) being absorbed through the mucosa of the intestinal walls and on into the bloodstream.

An individual's digestive processes can be improved by an experienced practitioner. Bio-individuality is a major factor in prescribing a course of treatment in cases of malfunctioning digestion. There are many variables to consider. Some patients, we find, have under-active stomachs and others have a lack of bile production. Many have a combination of them all. As we grow older, and especially from the fifth decade onwards, a reduction in the production of digestive ferments (especially stomach acids) becomes very common.

Fortunately, there are many very effective remedies for improving the various digestive malfunctions. These include supplying the missing enzymes in tablet form; stimulating the glands themselves to work more productively; soothing the often inflamed mucosa of the intestine; replacing the vital intestinal flora; altering the pH (acid/alkaline balance) of the large bowel and the stomach; and adding vital nutrients that rebuild the walls and other tissue connected with the gastro-intestinal tract.

Probably the single most important measure we take to improve the 'internal environment' (a phrase coined by

Professor Roger Williams of Texas University — the discoverer of vitamin B5) is meal reversal, which is described on page 33.

We have seen literally thousands of remarkable improvements in health following attention to the simple procedure of meal reversal. This is because our bodies are designed to function within a definite time-pattern.

This pattern was first discovered (in the Western world) by Professor Kurt Richter, the famous American bio-psychologist, who died at the age of ninety-four in January 1989.

In 1927 Kurt Richter discovered the bio-rhythm principle that governs body function. From his early work has grown the new science of bio-chronology which seeks to understand and utilise our body's time clock to improve health and performance.

How do you know if you have allergies?

Any otherwise unexplained illness, depletion in energy levels, or psychological problem should be suspected as being caused by a metabolic intolerance or allergic reaction.

Below is a list of common allergy symptoms.

PHYSICAL SYMPTOMS

Head: headaches, faintness, dizziness, feeling of fullness in the head, excessive drowsiness or sleepiness soon after eating, insomnia.

Eyes, ears, nose and throat: runny nose, stuffy nose, excessive mucus formation, watery eyes, blurring of vision, ringing of the ears, fluid in the middle ear, ear drainage, sore throats, chronic cough, gagging, canker sores, itching of the roof of the mouth, recurrent sinusitis.

Heart and lungs: palpitations, rapid heart rate (tachycardia), asthma, congestion in the chest, hoarseness, tickling cough.

Gastro-intestinal: nausea, vomiting, diarrhoea, constipation, malabsorption, bloating after meals, belching, colitis, flatulance (passing of gas), feeling of fullness in the stomach long after finishing a meal, abdominal pains or cramps, Crohn's disease, irritable bowel.

Skin: hives, rashes, eczema, dermatitis, pallor, peteclisae (small red freckle-like spots)

Other symptoms: chronic fatigue, weakness, muscle aches and pains, joint aches and pains, swelling of the hands, feet or ankles, urinary tract symptoms (frequency, urgency), vaginal itching, vaginal discharge, hunger (and its close ally, binge or spree eating), excessive reactions to temperature changes.

PSYCHOLOGICAL SYMPTOMS:

Anxiety panic attacks, depression, crying jags, aggressive behaviour, irritability, mental dullness, mental lethargy, confusion, excessive daydreaming, hyperactivity, restlessness, learning disabilities, poor work habits, slurred speech, stuttering, inability to concentrate, indifference, impaired judgement, clumsiness, memory loss.

Note: More serious mental illness such as schizophrenia can also sometimes be caused by food/chemical sensitivity. (See *Chemical Victims* by Dr Richard Mackarness, a psychologist-ecologist, published by Pan Books.)

Causes of Allergies

All manner of things in the environment can cause allergies or sensitivities. Here is a list of factors:

Physical Factors: These include heat, cold, weather cycles, positive and negative ions, electromagnetic radiation (including light), noise, and ionising radiation (radioactivity).

Chemical Factors: These include (a) inorganic substances, such as lead, mercury, cadmium, aluminium, arsenic, asbestos, chlorine, beryllium, nickel, copper, and many others; (b) organic substances, among which some of the more common toxic ones are formaldehyde, benzenes, toluene, xylene, and many other substances derived from gas and oil, chlorinated compounds, including organochlorine pesticides, PCBs; herbicides; pesticides like pyrethrins and malathion etc.

Foods: Especially those most commonly eaten in a community; dairy products — and others foreign to the human digestive tract (for which we have no digestive enzymes); foods high in alkaloids (chocolate, tea, coffee); foods high in aromatics (strong tasting or smelling); foods high in certain natural chemicals of other types, as salycilates (all fruits, tomato, capsicum, zucchini, cucumber, gherkin, chili, baked beans; almonds; honey; most herbs and spices).

Biological Factors: Fungi — such as moulds, dusts, pollens, animal dandruff, bacteria etc.

How did I become Allergic?

If you have reached adulthood (and may have been there for quite a while!) without these symptoms, you may wonder why they begin to creep in or may suddenly be there?

The answer may lie in what is called the 'total load' (on your immune system). If you liken your immune system to a camel (as Dr William Crook does in his wonderful book *The Yeast Connection*, Oidium Books, 1983) and you imagine placing various stresses such as poor diet, lack of sleep, social tensions, overwork on the camel's back, then you can see quite clearly the 'straw principle' at work. The 'last straw', the one that breaks the camel's back, is the one that causes the immune system's defence to be breached. Fortunately, the principle works quite well in reverse. By removing one or two straws, the immune system very often bounces back. Even though there may be quite a load on your immune system, it is usually very resilient and forgiving.

However, for many chronically ill sensitivity patients the load has been there for too long — and these people are often destined to a lifelong battle as a result of their compromised immunity.

The secret is to listen to your body, to pay attention to its ups-and-downs (without becoming a hypochondriac or super-anxious about your health). Just take note of unusual symptoms that persist. **Do not always blame something else — like aging or other circumstances**: sensitivity, reaction to foods, is often the first early warning sign that you have been overdoing things or compromising your health in some other way.

Consult an environmental practitioner with experience in allergic sensitivities. He or she will firstly exclude other unpleaseant possibilities before targeting your problem, if it is indeed sensitivity to the environment, and will explain how it came about.

Sometimes very simple things can begin a train of events that leads to an acute breakdown of immune ability.

I recently saw a patient who, although seemingly fit and full of energy, had suddenly collapsed one day after going for his daily swim and had been rushed to hospital.

It turned out that for the past year or more he had been having ten sugarfree cola drinks daily, plus ten cups of tea. This equals a caffeine intake of 700 mg a day – about three medicinal doses daily – and had been having this seven days a week for eighteen months.

This amazing intake of caffeine had continually stimulated his adrenal glands (which is why he felt full of energy all the time) until at last they had 'burned-out'. The 'total load point' had been reached. Since that episode, he had become sensitive to many foods and chemicals.

Fortunately, sudden episodes of extensive breakdown are not the most usual way of discovering sensitivity problems. Usually there is a period of time in which a variety of symptoms begin to appear. This time lapse before serious problems begin can take anything from days to several years. Early signs include: weakness; excessive tiredness; swelling of hands, feet or eyes; spots before the eyes; lethargy after meals; memory loss; irritability; a yellowing skin; oily hair; cracking or 'chipping' fingernails; changing sleep patterns; flatulence; bloating; indigestion; intolerance to things once benign to you (such as alcohol, chemicals and medication).

It is at the appearance of these early signs that you should take action and seek professional advice. This way you may be able to save yourself a lot of trouble!

Note: If you are seeking a doctor or naturopath who understands allergy sensitivities, candida, and similar problems consult our list of contacts on page 131.

Not all in the Stomach

We have said a lot about the effects of foods on health and suggested that taking away the allergens may help many health problems. However, we must never forget the powerful role of the mind on our health. A landmark series of studies at the New York Hospital and Cornell University (Drs Harold and Stewart Wolf) showed how our mental attitude can cause the stomach, and digestion, to slow right down, to become congested and fragile and in depression to become pale and covered with mucus.

The person driven by his or her emotions, about ten per cent of the population, is susceptible to some bleeding in the stomach when confronted with frustration and other forms of emotional block; from this can begin the common peptic ulcer and its accompanying problems.

When continued for a period of time mental and emotional problems and negative attitudes will tend to bring on changes in the internal environment that lead to allergies.

This, then, is another side of the allergy story which needs a different prescription for prevention. However, no matter how the allergies arose in the first place, applying the principles in this book should certainly help to relieve the symptoms.

Home and Other Treatment for Candidiasis

On page 12 of this book, Dr Mackarness describes general steps to solve the candida problem. In addition, the following specific methods are regularly used by naturopaths:

i. Enhancement of friendly mucous membrane bacterial population

The 'wet' surfaces of the human gastro-intestinal tract (GIT) and all other 'wet' surfaces (mouth, vagina, etc), are called mucous membranes.

They play host to a population of bacteria weighing a total average of 1½ kilos. At 10 billion or so per gram, this equates to 1500 x 10 billion!

This population is vital to our mucous membrane health. It is an 'ethnic' mix of some 300 species, of which some 10 per cent are 'unfriendly'. This 10 per cent includes candida.

The friendly bacteria are powerful antibiotics, and in sufficient numbers can deal with such enemies as gastro-enteritis bacteria and candida. These friendly bacteria include acidopholus and bifidus strains.

It is these friendly bacteria that are depleted by antibiotics (along with pathogens) and other stress factors, including poor diet. They must be reinforced.

Method: Ask your practitioner for a reliable brand of acidopholus and bifidus bacterial.

Drink a teaspoon of acidopholus in warm, pure water 20 minutes before meals for a week. Repeat monthly until well.

Use a half-teaspoon as a vaginal douche in pure warm water (it is good for *all* vaginal problems) twice daily for a week.

Use Bifidus, one teaspoon twice daily, in warm water as a retention enema (retain in rectum).

To do this, obtain a 50 ml catheter-tipped syringe and rectal tube from a chemist. Mix Bifidus into a slurry with about 20 ml warm pure water. Place rectal tube on end of syringe and insert about 8 cm (3") of the tube, lubricated with vegetable oil, into back passage. Plunge the plunger and retain the slurry.

ii. Use of 465 Hz audio frequency

Every living thing has its own vibratory rate (humans vibrate at about 8.7 Hz). By increasing this natural vibratory rate expotentially it is possible to destroy simple organisms like single cell yeast-forms yet not effect the host. Candida albicans vibrates at 465 Hz. You can find practitioners who use Frequency Therapy for systemic (through-the-body) candidiasis. Ring National Bioenergetic Medicine Association — (075) 38 2496.

Michael Sichel ND, DO

THE CANDIDA DIET

During the first few days on your candidiasis programme you may experience withdrawal symptoms from cessation of allergic foods. Symptoms can include headaches, nausea, lethargy, constipation or diarrhoea.

FOODS TO AVOID

All sugars and fruits*
All types! No raw sugar, honey, or foods containing sugar (such as commercial juices, cordials, breakfast cereals, etc). **Read the labels on all foods!**

Malted foods*
Such as sweets with malt, Horlicks, malted breakfast cereals, etc.

Fermented beverages†
Especially beer and wine, whisky, brandy, gin, rum, vodka, cider, etc.

Ferments/moulds†
Soya sauce, vegemite, promite, marmite, miso, mushrooms. Other foods with mould include, cantaloupes, melons, oranges, dried fruits of all kinds (raisins, figs, prunes, etc), pickled and smoked foods (especially frankfurters), corned beef, devon, etc. Also stale or stored foods (packet foods left open must be eaten fresh). Canned juices, especially tomato and apple.

Raised (yeasted) breads and doughs†	Breads, buns, rolls, pastries, biscuits (except those allowed under 'Food to Eat'), cakes, cake mixes, etc.
Vinegars†	Including salad dressing (use lemon juice instead), mayonnaise, pickles, olives, most sauces of all kinds including chili, pickled beets, relishes, etc.
Dairy products†	Everything from the cow — milk, cream, matured cheese, butter, buttermilk, sour cream, etc. (Some very fresh, less than 3 days old, milk may be used by some patients — sparingly).
Brewers yeast†	No type of yeast (including torula) or vitamins containing yeast.
Stored nuts†	Especially peanuts, but freshly shelled nuts are all right. No peanut butter.
Coffee, tea and cola drinks†	

Do not take antibiotics

* Foods that feed candida.
† Foods to which a person with candidiasis will be allergic, although they do not actually feed candida.

FOODS TO EAT (food marked * are protein foods)
The following either kill or inhibit candida:
raw garlic, onion, kale, turnips, cabbage, horseradish and broccoli.

All vegetables
Young lean meat (if meat eater)*
Free range chicken*
Fish*
Free range eggs*
Legumes of all kinds (soya beans, lentils, lima, barlotti, navy beans)*
Small amounts of brown rice and other wholegrain unyeasted foods (e.g. Ryvita, Vitaweet, rice cakes, waffles made from wholegrains and buckwheat (see recipe p 116), Matzo (Jewish) unleavened bread, millet biscuits and wholegrain freshly ground porridge, etc. Carbohydrates (of which the above grain foods mostly consist) in small amounts: including full grain rye bread, yeast-free Demeter bread, potatoes, pasta (especially wholegrain spaghetti, etc)
Goats milk products, sugar free soya milk, plain yoghurt (Attiki Acidopholis is possible)*
Herb teas, dandelion coffee etc
Nuts and seeds (such as sunflower, sesame) and tahini paste*
Homemade salad dressings (with lemon and garlic, etc)
Some grapefruit and lemon allowed
Any packaged foods should be eaten freshly opened
Tinned fish (eaten freshly opened)*, homemade soups/broths (eat fresh), popcorn, twice baked bread ('Zweibak'), in fact, almost all foods not in the 'Foods to Avoid' list.

Make sure you eat enough! If you cut out foods you must replace them adequately.

Note on diet
Remember that this diet is not 'for the term of your natural life'! (Although it is nutritionally very sound and many well informed vegetarians live long lives on this programme — without the chicken and also sometimes without the fish.)

But for one month, at least, this diet should be adhered to strictly. Severe and chronic sufferers will have to remain on the diet longer.

Withdrawals: If you have been a consistent coffee or tea drinker you may experience headaches and/or nausea for a day or so. Try to dilute your particular drink, gradually diluting further and adding dandelion coffee or similar to the coffee, or peppermint tea or similar to the tea.

Possible allergens among the above

Some patients will find trouble with foods that are normally acceptable to other allergy victims. This is because of biological individuality. Below is a short list of some of the most common allergens:

- deadly nightshade family (such as tomatoes, potatoes)
- salicylate family (all fruits except skinned pears), plus tomatoes, capsicum, zucchini, cucumber, gherkin, chili, baked beans
- almonds, honey, most herbs and spices
- carrots, oranges, bananas and tinned fruit

Research studies over a period of several decades show that those who live or work in closed spaces and in environments containing more positive airborne ions than negative ions (such as air-conditioned buildings) may develop a variety of symptoms. Typical manifestations include fatigue, headache, drowsiness, irritability, nasal discharge, burning eyes and coughing. These and other symptoms commonly found in individuals with yeast-connected health disorders may be helped by a negative ion generator.

EASY TO FOLLOW DAILY EATING PROGRAMME

On arising
2–3 glasses of water (filtered or rain if possible) in which you have soaked slices of lemon (including skin) overnight. Add hot water to make warm.

Main meal — Breakfast (rather than dinner). This meal reversal is most important for all digestive tract problems.

- Choose one recipe from Salads.
- One from Protein Dishes or Fish. Those who retain meat in the diet can also have it at this meal and should certainly have it no later than lunchtime.
- One from Vegetables.
- One from Staple Dishes.

Those working, who can't manage a meal like this, do at least have protein and some raw vegetables before leaving for work. This is important.

Lunch
- Choose from Salads.
- One from Grains and Desserts.

Evening meal (this should be light)
- Choose one from Soups.
- One from Salads.
- Crispbread such as Kavli, Ryvita, Matzo or Sesame Crackers or Scottish Oatcakes (see page 124).

Comments on Daily Eating Programme

The suggested menu has been scientifically compiled. The reasons for making breakfast your main meal are:
- The peak performance of your stomach is between 7.00

and 9.00 am (between 5.00 and 7.00 pm is the peak performance of the kidneys).

- The body is most active after breakfast, until about 3.00 pm, when it begins to slow down. This includes the digestive tract as well as every other system. Therefore thetransit time of the food you have eaten at breakfast is likely to be shorter, which is important, particularly with putrefactive foods, such as meat and other proteins, and also cooked food.
- Your blood sugar level is below normal on arising. If you do not eat any breakfast it will stay at this lowered rate, and you will be working on your reserves.

    If you eat the usual high carbohydrate, sweet breakfast, even fruit, the blood sugar will rise quickly, but will then drop rapidly and be below normal again. With this sudden drop in blood sugar you will also feel a lack of energy, tiredness, and a desire for something sweet by morning tea time. If you have protein for breakfast, combined with raw or slightly cooked vegetables, you will not have this problem. We have had many patients suffering from hypoglycaemia (low blood sugar) in our clinic. They have done very well on this breakfast.

    It is easier for candida patients to resist eating sweets and fruits if eating a *good protein breakfast and nothing sweet*.
- Because your body is active earlier in the day, having your main meal for breakfast fits in very well with a weight control diet. The food metabolises better and you will be less inclined to 'pick' in between meals, since a normal bood sugar level will prevent you from feeling hungry.

Reasons for making your evening meal light are:

- Your body is tired after a day's work; this includes your stomach. It is not wise to eat large heavy meals when tired. Very often the food just sits in the stomach all night, often causing colic.
- The body has slowed down, as has the digestive system. It will therefore take much longer to digest a meal, especially a heavy meal, such as meat and cooked vegetables.

- When going to bed with a full stomach and food only half digested, you will have a restless, poor quality sleep. This affects your nervous system adversely. To have a good quality sleep the stomach should be empty and at rest, the same as the rest of the body.
- A large heavy meal with no activity or very little after it, tends to cause weight problems. It will also cause constipation, the root of many chronic diseases.
- When you have eaten a large heavy meal at night, you will feel lethargic on waking and you will not be ready for a proper breakfast. It is like a hangover.

To switch over to this menu it is wise to start making the evening meal lighter first and then gradually increasing your breakfast. It takes time to change the routine, especially if you are the cook. Plan your breakfast the day before. Make casseroles or patty mixes, which can be stored in the fridge or freezer, ready to cook in the morning. Tossed salads can be kept in airtight containers or similar if necessary.

Once you have planned everything this way you will feel the freedom of not having to rush home to cook a meal when you are out somewhere, and you don't tire yourselves out cooking at the end of the day, then eating and then having to do the dishes. But, most important of all, the health of the family will improve.

Gastrointestinal Peak Times in Bio-chronology

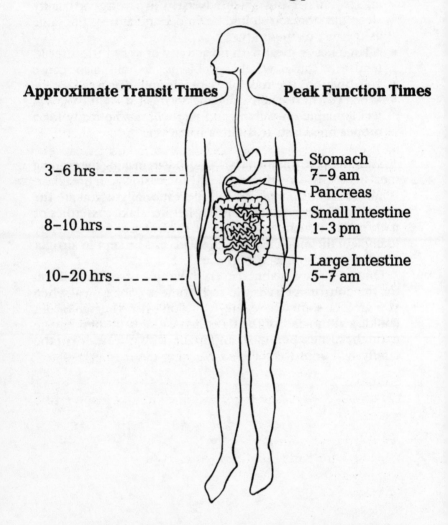

Approximate Transit Times

3–6 hrs

8–10 hrs

10–20 hrs

Peak Function Times

Stomach
7–9 am
Pancreas
Small Intestine
1–3 pm

Large Intestine
5–7 am

Professor Kurt Richter, an American psycho-biologist, discovered the bio-rhythm timing of various organs in the late 1920s. Oriental medicine had by that time already been using this knowledge for thousands of years!

SEVEN DAY STEP-BY-STEP MENU PLAN

U sing the seven day menu is a good way to get started on the candida diet. It is designed to commence on Sunday, so that you have time to shop and make preparations on Saturday, rather than trying to start the diet in the middle of the week, which is for most people a more hectic time. The diet can be modified to suit individual needs and tastes.

Saturday before starting menu plan
Prepare for Sunday:
Soak mung beans overnight
Coleslaw (put in airtight container in fridge)
Scottish Oatcakes, if necessary

Buy necessary vegetables for Sunday and Monday
Where you have little time for preparations during the weekdays, it is all right to make a number of protein dishes during the weekend to keep in the freezer. Take out the casserole wanted for the next morning the evening before.

Sunday
On arising 2–3 glasses warm lemon drink (see daily eating programme)

Breakfast (main meal)
Fried Rice (or barley if allergic to rice)
Mung Beans
Coleslaw
Sugar Snap Peas

Lunch
Cornmeal Pancakes or Waffles or Pikelets
Salmon Toss

Evening Meal (light)
Pumpkin Soup
Scottish Oatcakes or crispbread
alfalfa sprouts with cold pressed oil

Prepare for Monday:
Easy Bread
Sesame Crackers
Barlotti Bean Loaf

Monday
On arising 2–3 glasses warm lemon drink

Breakfast
Spiced Potatoes
Barlotti Bean Loaf
Spinach Salad
Brussel Sprouts

Lunch
Easy Bread
pumpernickel (very dark thinly sliced rye bread)
Waldorf Salad

Evening Meal
Celery Soup
Sesame Crackers
mixed sprouts in cold pressed oil

Prepare for Tuesday:
Buy necessary vegetables
Beetroot Salad

Tuesday
On arising 2–3 glasses warm lemon drink

Breakfast
Barley and Spinach Pasta
Marinated Grilled Fish

Peas and Carrots
Beetroot Salad

Lunch
some Hors d'Oeuvres bites
Sour Dough Bread
matzos
almonds

Dinner
Red Lentil Soup
variety of crispbread
bean sprouts in cold pressed oil

Prepare for Wednesday:
Buy necessary vegetables
Lentil Patty mixture
Green Bean Salad except for yoghurt

Wednesday
On arising 2 glasses warm lemon drink

Breakfast
Buckwheat Roast
Lentil Patties
Broccoli
Green Bean Salad

Lunch
Radish Salad
Milk Porridge
Scones
pepitas

Dinner
Beetroot Soup
crispbread
small Butternut Salad

Prepare for Thursday:
Buy necessary vegetables
Chick Pea Casserole
Red Cabbage Salad
Easy Bread

Thursday
On arising 2 glasses warm lemon drink

Breakfast
Potato Pancakes
Chick Pea Casserole
Cauliflower
Red Cabbage Salad

Lunch
Carrot Salad
Easy Bread
pecan nuts

Dinner
Vegetable Soup
Scottish Oatcakes, matzos
alfalfa sprouts with cold pressed oil

Prepare for Friday:
Buy necessary vegetables
Beetroot Salad
Cornbread Cakes
Soak cannelini beans overnight

Friday
On arising 2 glasses warm lemon drink

Breakfast
Savoury Millet
Ovenbaked Ocean Bream
Beetroot Salad
Sugar Snap Peas and Baby Carrots

Lunch
Hors d'Oeuvres bites
Corn Bread Cakes
pumpernickel

Dinner
Cannelini Bean Soup
crispbread
mixed sprouts with cold pressed oil

Prepare for Saturday:
Buy necessary vegetables
Nut Galatine
Pumpkin Pie
Rice Salad
Asparagus Salad (cover in food wrap)
Sesame Crackers (if necessary)

Saturday
On arising 2 glasses warm lemon drink
Breakfast
Potato Casserole
Asparagus Salad
Nut Galatine
Red Cabbage

Lunch
Rice Salad
Pumpkin Pie or Carob Pudding

Dinner
Choko Soup or Spinach Soup
Sesame Crackers
Parsnip Salad (small)

Prepare for Sunday:
Buy necessary vegetables for Sunday and Monday
Prepare planned casseroles and salads and also baking

PRODUCT INFORMATION

agar agar

A natural jelly derived from the sea.

artificial sweetener

Use sparingly and try to obtain the most natural powder, not containing cyclamate or aspartame.

barley flour

Obtainable at health food stores. Use for thickening soups and sauces.

basil, fresh

Best grown with tomatoes to keep off bugs.

basil, dried

Has a flavour like black pepper, but not the harmful effect that pepper has on the stomach lining.

bay leaf

Apart from flavouring soups and stews it stops flatulence.

cloves

Same effect as bay leaf.

cold pressed oil (preferably olive oil, see note p 46)

This oil is not extracted by using heat, neither are any chemicals used in the process of extraction. Some are very rich in linoleic acid, a necessary substance for digestion. Heated oils, especially twice heated oils, are carcinogenic (can cause cancer).

cottage cheese

This is easier to digest than milk or usual cheeses. All soured milk products are easier to digest because of bacterial action.

A number of allergy patients cannot tolerate even these dairy foods because of their lactose content.

egg replacer (Orgran)
Obtainable at health food stores. Use 1 heaped teaspoon mixed with 2 tablespoons water to replace *one* egg.

garlic
Blackmore's 'Garlix' is a superior way of taking garlic without tasting it. 'Garlix' is freeze dried and contains the important antibiotic properties of garlic.

goat's milk
Easier to digest than cow's milk and much healthier, but not tolerated by some allergy patients.

health curry
Bolst mild curry paste, obtainable at the deli or health food stores. Some people are allergic to this curry as well.

kombu
A seaweed vegetable which is now hard to obtain. Can be left out of recipe.

low allergy baking powder
Obtainable at health food stores. It does not have the harmful ingredients in other baking powders and agrees with most people suffering from allergies.

modified butter
This is not available in shops. To make it, blend 1 cup of cold pressed oil with 1¼ cups of cold water until creamy, then add

250 g (½ lb) butter bit by bit. It is spreadable straight out of the fridge and is the answer for those on a low cholesteral diet rather than carcinogenic margarines.

pepitas	Green pumpkin seeds with a nutty taste. Obtainable at health food stores.
rice flour	Use for thickening soups and sauces as well as for baking. Obtainable at health food stores.
soft butter	This is also a form of modified butter, but not quite as good. Available in shops.
sour cream	See cottage cheese.
soya mayonnaise	A dairy-free mayonnaise obtainable at health food stores.
soya milk	A non-dairy substitute for milk.
tahini	Sesame paste which can be used as a bread spread or in casserole dishes. Available from health food stores.
tofu	Soya been cheese. Cut in ½ cm (¼ ") slices and marinade in a mixture of Maggi seasoning and water overnight. Fry both sides until brown.
tumeric	A yellow powdered herb with a curry-like flavour. If you are not allergic to this it is a good substitute for curry. To make it hot you'll need to add cayenne pepper as well.

TVP	Textured Vegetable Protein, made from soya beans. Some added ingredients could be allergenic.
water purifier	Drinking treated tap water will hinder your progress. Chlorine, which is contained in all town water, has a very bad effect on your intestinal flora. A healthy intestinal flora is extremely important for candida patients and also for other patients suffering from serious or not so serious illnesses. A water purifier is a very good health investment.
wheatgerm	This is part of the wheat. If allergic to this, maybe rolled millet can be substituted for it.
yoghurt	Make sure you get a good continental quality. It is a very healthy food for those who can tolerate it.

Important note on cooking oil

Most cooking oils produce oxidants when heated. Oxidants are precursors to many diseases including cancer. Olive oil is an exception; it is a monosaturated fat and so has reduced peroxide production. Use of garlic or onion in cooking oil reduces oxidant risk.

Margarine also contains large amounts of heated oil. See the Modified Butter recipe on page 44.

Supplements

Spirulina: This is a single-cell microalgae that grows in warm fresh water. It is the single most nutritious food source known to man and richest of any wholefood in the following organic immune-boosting nutrients:

1. Beta-carotene: A powerful anti-oxidant that protects all other anti-oxidants (substances that cause disease processes and ageing). *The Journal of Nutrition*, July 1989, published a study showing organic beta-carotene to have a 10-fold higher assimilation and biological activity than synthetic beta-carotene.

Currently, the average intake of beta-carotene is only 2 mg daily. In the US, the National Cancer Institute is now recommending 6 mg as the minimum daily requirement. This is because b-c has been shown in very large population studies to protect against cancer of the lung and other cancers.

New studies show that it can restore the communication pathways between cell walls that transmit 'normal growth' signals. It can thus normalise abnormal cell growth.

'Lifestream Spirulina' — a brand that is used by most practitioners and is available from health food stores, gives you about 12 mg on an average daily dose.

2. Iron: Population studies in the Western world invariably show that very high percentages of women suffer from mild to severe iron deficiency. Spirulina is 10 per cent iron, the highest source, by far, of any food. Moreover, it is organic iron, 94 per cent assimilable and will not cause constipation — as many iron supplements do.

3. B12: Spirulina has more than four times that found in beef liver.

4. Calcium: Twice as much as in sesame seeds or parsley — the closest rivals.

5. Amino Acids: Twice as rich as soya beans in protein, spirulina is 60 per cent higher quality protein.

Ultradophilus and Ultrabifidus

These two living foods possess unique abilities to enhance natural immunity, restore health in both the small and large intestine and supply B vitamins.

They are made by Metagenics and must be stored in the refrigerator to preserve their guaranteed billion-plus organisms per gram population.

Probioplex: Is an antibody concentrate (US patented) made from whey. It eliminates over 40 intestinal pathogenic organisms responsible for diarrhoea and mucosal inflammations. Probioplex also helps the friendly bacteria, like acidopholus and bifidus, to adhere to your bowel walls and colonise.

Probioplex also enhances the activity of these friendly bacteria in eliminating candida albicans and other enemies.

SHOPPING GUIDE

Health food store
cold pressed oil
mung beans
mixed nuts
vegetable salt
light health curry
rice or barley flour
rye flour
soya flour
buckwheat flour
fine millet flour
fine cornmeal
rolled barley or
barley flakes
sesame seeds
tofu

celery seeds
wheatgerm
ground linseed
sunflower kernels
soya milk
soya mayonnaise
plain yoghurt
kombu (seaweed)
TVP
spinach vermicelli or mie
carob powder
agar agar
tahini
pepitas

Deli
pumpernickel
matzos
crispbread

Supermarket
Maggi seasoning
peas (frozen or fresh)
gherkins

salmon
tuna
buttermilk

Health food stores or supermarket
cinnamon
chervil
all spice

paprika
nutmeg
basil

cayenne pepper
oregano
bay leaves
pure vanilla
unpolished brown
   rice
potassium
   bicarbonate
cloves
thyme
horseradish paste
Greek olives
anchovy paste
walnuts
rolled oats
crispbread
red lentils
brown lentils

kidney beans
cannelini beans
lima beans
haricot beans
soya beans
chick peas
goat's milk
wholemeal flour
tumeric
dill tips
ground coriander
cream of tartar
arrowroot
artificial sweeteners
containing no
   sorbitol, aspartame or
   cyclamate

Opposite: Vegetable Soup (page 53) and Red Lentil Soup (page 58)
Overleaf: Zucchini Salad and Beetroot Salad (page 71)

SOUPS

Vegetable Soup

variety of vegetables such as: carrots, peas,
   beans, cauliflower, parsley, celery, leeks,
   etc.
1¼ litres (2 pints) water
¼ cup cooked brown rice or vermicelli
2 tablespoons cold pressed oil
¼ teaspoon nutmeg
¼ teaspoon dried basil
pinch cayenne pepper

Wash vegetables and cut into small pieces. Sauté in oil for 10
minutes. Add water and rice or vermicelli and simmer for 30
minutes. Add the herbs to taste.

Potato Soup

4 potatoes (or sweet potatoes)
¾ litre (1¼ pints) water
1 cup goat's milk or soya milk
1 teaspoon cold pressed oil
1 cup chopped leeks
¼ cup coarsely grated carrot
¼ cup chopped celery (including leaves)
Maggi seasoning to taste
pinch cayenne pepper
½ teaspoon nutmeg

Scrub potatoes, cut in pieces, including skin, and cook in water until soft. Put potatoes and remaining cooking liquid through a strainer and add milk. Sauté vegetables in oil with Maggi seasoning, cayenne pepper and nutmeg for about 10 minutes and add to the potatoes.

Sweetcorn Soup

1 onion, finely chopped
1 clove garlic, crushed
1 tablespoon cold pressed oil
2 tablespoons rice flour
1 litre water
1 cup sweetcorn, mashed
1 egg yolk, beaten (optional)
Maggi seasoning to taste
¼ cup chopped parsley
2 tablespoons yoghurt (optional)

Sauté onion and garlic in hot oil until onion is transparent. Add rice flour and gradually stir in half the water. Add egg yolk, corn and Maggi seasoning and simmer for 10 minutes. Just before serving add parsley and yoghurt.

Spinach Soup

2 cups finely shredded spinach
¾ litre (1¼ pints) water
1 tablespoon cold pressed olive oil
1 onion, chopped
2 tablespoons rice flour
½ cup goat's milk or soya milk
pinch cayenne pepper
1 teaspoon dried basil
½ teaspoon nutmeg
Maggi seasoning to taste
rice snaps, for serving

Wash and cook spinach in 1 cup of water for about 5 minutes on low heat. Put through blender, retaining any remaining cooking liquid. Heat oil, sauté onion until transparent, then add flour and remaining water while constantly stirring. Add spinach and other ingredients. Simmer for 10 minutes and serve with rice snaps.

Carrot Soup

1 onion
1 tablespoon cold pressed oil
2 tablespoons rice or barley flour
¾ litre (1¼ pints) water
½ cup cooked mashed carrots
½ cup peas
1 cup of goat's milk or soya milk
Maggi seasoning to taste
pinch cayenne pepper
1 teaspoon dried basil
½ teaspoon oregano
¼ cup finely chopped parsley

Chop onion and sauté in hot oil until transparent. Using French whisk, add flour while gradually adding water. Add other ingredients and simmer for 10 minutes. Lastly add finely chopped parsley.

Celery Soup

1 onion
1 cup chopped celery
1 tablespoon cold pressed oil
3 tablespoons rice flour
¾ litre (1¼ pints) water
¼ cup goat's milk or soya milk
Maggi seasoning
¼ cup chopped celery leaves
2-3 tablespoons of yoghurt

Chop onion and sauté with celery in hot oil until onion transparent. Using a French whisk, add flour and gradually stir in the water. Simmer until celery is soft. Strain if required. Add milk, Maggi seasoning and celery leaves. Before serving stir in yoghurt.

Tomato Soup

3-4 tomatoes (unsprayed if possible)
1 small bay leaf
2 cloves
¾ litre (1¼ pints) water
1 onion
1 tablespoon cold pressed oil
2 tablespoons rice or barley flour
1 cup goat's or soya milk
pinch of cayenne pepper
2 tablespoons fresh basil, chopped
2 tablespoons parsley or celery leaves
vegetable salt to taste
2 tablespoons yoghurt

Simmer tomatoes with bay leaf and cloves in some of the water until soft. Put through strainer, retaining any remaining cooking liquid. Chop onion and sauté until transparent. Add flour and then gradually add the remaining water while stirring. Add the milk, cayenne, basil and parsley or celery leaves. Salt to taste. Simmer for a few minutes and add yoghurt before serving.

Red Lentil Soup

½ cup red lentils
1 carrot, coarsely grated
1 litre (1½ pints) water
1 bay leaf
1 onion
1 tablespoon of safflower oil
little thyme and tumeric
Maggi seasoning
squeeze lemon juice
seaweed or plain rice snaps, for serving.

Cook lentils and carrot in the water with the bay leaf for 15 minutes or until soft. Chop onion and sauté in hot oil with herbs for 10 minutes. Add to the lentils along with the rest of water and other ingredients. Simmer for about ½ hour. Serve with seaweed or plain rice snaps.

Kidney Bean Soup

½ cup kidney beans or barlotti beans
1 litre (1½ pints) water
3 cloves
1 bay leaf
1 large onion
1 leek
1 celery stalk with leaves, chopped
1 tablespoon cold pressed oil
1· teaspoon tumeric
½ teaspoon thyme
½ teaspoon nutmeg
1 teaspoon dried basil
pinch cayenne pepper
1 tablespoon rice flour or barley flour
Maggi seasoning to taste
vegetable salt to taste

Soak beans in the water for 24 hours with cloves and bay leaf.
Cook them until soft, then mash them or use blender. Chop
and sauté onion, leeks and celery stalks in hot oil for about
10 minutes. Add to the beans the herbs, spices and rice or barley
flour, Maggi seasoning, salt and chopped celery leaves. Simmer
for 15 minutes.

Cannelini Bean Soup

½ cup cannelini or haricot beans
1 litre (1½ pints) water
1 onion
1 leek
1 tablespoon cold pressed oil
1 tablespoon rice or barley flour
Maggi seasoning to taste
vegetable salt to taste
½ teaspoon nutmeg
pinch cayenne pepper

Soak beans in water for 24 hours. Bring to boil, and cook for about 1½ hours or until soft. Chop onion and leeks and sauté in hot oil for a few minutes. Add together with barley or rice flour to the beans, add Maggi seasoning, salt, nutmeg and cayenne pepper. Simmer till creamy.

Pumpkin Soup

2 cups diced butternut pumpkin
  (including skin)
¾ litre (1¼ pints) water
1 cup goat's or soya milk
1 small onion
1 tablespoon cold pressed oil
2 tablespoons rice or barley flour
Maggi seasoning to taste
1 teaspoon dried basil
½ teaspoon nutmeg
pinch cayenne pepper
parsley, very finely chopped
1 tablespoon yoghurt

Cook pumpkin in the water until soft, then mash. Add rice or barley flour while stirring with French whisk. Sauté onion in hot oil for 10 minutes. Add together with herbs, Maggi seasoning and milk. Before serving on each plate add yoghurt.

Asparagus Soup

250 g (½ lb) asparagus
¾ litre (1¼ pints) water
1 tablespoon cold pressed oil
2 tablespoons rice or barley flour
1 egg yolk (optional)
1 cup goat's or soya milk
½ teaspoon nutmeg
Maggi seasoning
2 tablespoons yoghurt

Wash asparagus, cut off heads, cut stalks into small pieces and soak in half the water until soft. Rub through strainer, retaining any remaining liquid. Heat oil, add the flour and stir with French whisk or wooden spoon while adding the remaining water. Add the asparagus heads, then add other ingredients except the yoghurt. Simmer until asparagus heads are soft. Add yoghurt before serving.

Note: If fresh asparagus unavailable, use tinned asparagus cuts.

Beetroot Soup (borsch)

¾ litre (1¼ pints) water
1 beetroot, grated
1 carrot, grated
1 large onion, chopped
1 cup chopped celery
1 cup cooked lima or haricot beans
  (see page 81)
Maggi seasoning to taste
2 tablespoons chopped parsley
1 tablespoon fresh dill, chopped, or
  1 teaspoon dried dill tips
1 tablespoon lemon juice
2 tablespoons yoghurt

Bring water to boil with all ingredients except last four.
Simmer until soft, then add parsley, dill and lemon juice, stirring
in yoghurt just before serving.

Cucumber or Choko Soup

2 cups chopped cucumber or choko
¾ litre (1¼ pints) water
1 onion, chopped very finely
1 clove garlic, crushed
1 tablespoon cold pressed safflower oil
2 tablespoons rice or barley flour
½ cup goat's or soya milk
Maggi seasoning to taste
1 teaspoon lemon juice
1 tablespoon dill or 2 tablespoons parsley,
    chopped
2 tablespoons yoghurt

Cook cucumber or choko with some of the water till soft.
Blend and strain. Sauté onion and garlic in oil until onion
transparent, then, using French whisk, add rice or barley flour
and stir in remaining water and milk. Add Maggi seasoning and
lemon juice. Just before serving stir dill or parsley and yoghurt
through.

Summer Soup

½ cucumber
1 cup fresh peas
2-3 asparagus
1 spring onion
1 tablespoon cold pressed oil
2 tablespoons rice flour
¾ litre (1¼ pints) water
Maggi seasoning to taste
1 cup goat's or soya milk
2 tablespoons chopped fresh basil
2 tablespoons chopped parsley
squeeze of lemon juice

Finely chop vegetables and sauté in oil for 5 minutes. Add flour, then water gradually while stirring and then add Maggi seasoning. Simmer until vegetables are soft. Add milk, basil and parsley, then lemon juice and simmer for 5 minutes.

SALADS

Hors d'Oeuvres Platter

Rub garlic on platter before choosing some of the following:

- 5 cm (2") celery pieces filled with a mixture of cottage cheese and chives.
- 5 cm (2") celery pieces, made into curls by splitting down each side into thin sections, but leaving attached at base, then placing in iced water for about 1 hour.
- Carrots sliced lengthwise to make sticks.
- Radishes cut in slices, roses, quarters or used whole. Leave a few small middle leaves on and slice across bottom to stand up.
- Tomato slices or quarters. Put whole tomatoes in boiling water for a few minutes to be able to remove skin. Then slice or quarter and marinade in a mixture of cold pressed oil, lemon juice, basil and vegetable salt. Arrange on a platter. Top with finely chopped parsley.
- Cucumber slices. Marinade the same way as tomatoes.
- Sardines, slightly smoked or plain.
- Sliced cooked beetroot marinaded as tomatoes.
- Olives.

- Cottage cheese balls. Mix cottage cheese
  with a little yoghurt and grated nuts.
  Form into small balls using small spoon.

Serve before a meal with toasted bread fingers or dark Dutch
rye bread (pumpernickel) cut in long fingers.

Coleslaw

1 cup finely shredded cabbage
½ cup finely chopped celery
½ cup grated carrots
4 shallots, finely chopped
1 green apple, grated, or
    ½ cup finely chopped pineapple
1–2 tablespoons soya mayonnaise

Mix ingredients thoroughly.

Red Cabbage Salad

1 cup shredded red cabbage
½ cup finely chopped celery
4 shallots, finely chopped
1 green apple, grated
1–2 tablespoons soya mayonnaise

Mix ingredients together.

Spinach Salad

1½ cups finely shredded Chinese cabbage
1 green apple, grated
1 cup finely shredded spinach
1–2 tablespoons of cold pressed oil
squeeze of lemon juice

Mix ingredients together.

Carrot Salad

1 cup grated carrot
1 green apple, grated
¼ cup finely chopped celery
4 shallots, finely chopped
2–3 tablespoons ground sesame seeds
1–2 tablespoons cold pressed oil.

Mix ingredients together.

Radish Salad

lettuce or endive, finely shredded
3 radish, finely chopped
4 shallots, finely chopped
squeeze of lemon juice
1–2 tablespoons cold pressed oil

Mix ingredients together thoroughly.

Green Bean Salad

1 cup sliced cucumber
½ cup sliced green beans
2 cloves garlic, crushed
4 shallots, finely chopped
2–3 tablespoons yoghurt

Mix together with sufficient yoghurt to coat ingredients.

Waldorf Salad

1 cup finely chopped celery
2 green apples, finely diced
1 cup chopped walnuts
¼ cup cottage cheese
2–3 tablespoons yoghurt

Mix ingredients together.

Cauliflower Salad

¼ medium cauliflower
2 cups diced Granny Smith apples
¼ cup chopped walnuts
¼ cup finely chopped parsley
2 tablespoons yoghurt or sour cream

Remove hard stem off cauliflower. Wash and break into small pieces or slice thinly. Mix with the diced apple, walnuts, parsley and yoghurt or sour cream. Serve on torn lettuce leaves and decorate with radishes or tomato quarters.

Tomato Salad

1 cup chopped tomato (unsprayed if
   possible)
½ cup chopped cucumber
4 shallots, chopped
2 tablespoons chopped fresh basil
¼ cup sour cream or yoghurt

Mix ingredients together with either sour cream or yoghurt.

Zucchini Salad

1 cup chopped zucchini
1 tomato (unsprayed if possible), chopped
4 shallots, chopped
squeeze of lemon juice
2 tablespoons cold pressed oil

Mix ingredients together thoroughly. Serve with goat's or cottage cheese and Greek black olives.

Beetroot Salad

1 cup grated raw beetroot
½ cup finely chopped celery
4 shallots, finely chopped
1 medium-sized Granny Smith apple, grated
sour cream, for serving

Mix ingredients together and serve with sour cream.

Butternut Pumpkin Salad

1 cup finely grated butternut
½ cup walnut pieces
4 shallots, finely chopped
¼ cup chopped parsley
1 cup mixed bean sprouts or watercress
1-2 tablespoons cold pressed oil
1-2 radishes, sliced

Butternut should be grated very finely. Mix with walnut pieces, shallots, parsley and oil. Put mixture on a salad platter. Use sprouts or watercress to garnish by forming a ring around the edge of platter. Decorate with slices or radish.

Swede or Parsnip Salad

1 cup finely grated swede or parsnip
4–5 shallots, chopped
½ cup chopped celery
¼ cup continental parsley
1–2 tablespoons cold pressed oil
lettuce leaves, for serving

Mix ingredients together thoroughly. Serve on platter with torn lettuce leaves.

Asparagus Salad

12 asparagus spears
½ cup shredded Chinese cabbage
½ cup finely chopped celery
4 shallots, finely chopped
1 tablespoon soya mayonnaise
1–2 tomatoes (unsprayed if possible), sliced
½ cup olives

Arrange asparagus spears on platter like spokes of a wheel. Mix cabbage, celery and shallots with mayonnaise. Fill in between spokes. Decorate with tomato slices around edge of platter, retaining some tomato slices to place in middle together with olives.

Potato Salad

2 cups cubed cooked potatoes
¼ cup shallots or chives
3 gherkins
1 teaspoon dried basil
sour cream, to coat

Mix ingredients together thoroughly.

Note: Boiled eggs may be added too.

Rice Salad

2 cups cooked unpolished rice
1 medium-sized carrot, grated
½ cup chopped celery
½ cup chopped capsicum
5 gherkins, finely chopped
2–3 cups cubed fresh pineapple
¼ cup chopped shallots or chives
2 tablespoons fresh basil, chopped or
    1 tablespoon dried basil
2 teaspoon ground coriander seeds
lettuce leaves, for serving
1-2 tomatoes, sliced, for decorating
olives, for decorating
parsley sprigs, for decorating

**Mix ingredients together. Serve on bed of torn lettuce pieces.
Decorate according to taste with tomatoes, olives and parsley.**

Salmon Toss

1 large (220 g / 8 oz) tin salmon, drained and flaked
1 cucumber, sliced
1 cup chopped celery
¼ cup chopped spring onions
1 tablespoon soya mayonnaise
seasonings to taste
lettuce
tomatoes (unsprayed if possible),
    cut in wedges

**Combine salmon, cucumber, celery and spring onions. Pour
mayonnaise over and toss lightly. Season and chill.**

**Serve on a lettuce lined platter and garnish with tomato
wedges.**

Fish Salad

1 cup flaked fish
1 cup cooked rice
1 small Granny Smith apple
1-2 gherkins
½ teaspoon (to taste) horseradish paste or
    grated horseradish
vegetable salt, if necessary
1 teaspoon paprika
2-3 tablespoons soya mayonnaise
lettuce leaves, for serving

Mix fish and rice. Finely chop apple and gherkins and stir through the fish together with horseradish, salt, paprika and mayonnaise.

Serve on a bed of torn lettuce pieces.

FISH

Spicy Crumbed Sea Fish

2 teaspoons coriander
½ teaspoon ginger
½ cup wheatgerm
4 fish fillets
soya flour
1 egg lightly beaten with 1 tablespoon cold
   pressed oil
cold pressed oil, for shallow frying
shallots, for garnishing

Combine spices and wheatgerm. Flour fillets and dip in beaten egg. Coat in spicy crumb mixture and shallow fry till golden. Serve straight from pan. Garnish with shallots.

Fish Rissoles

1 large tin salmon, drained and flaked
1 cup mashed potato
1 small onion, finely chopped
2 tablespoons finely chopped parsley
½ teaspoon basil
little salt
1 egg
1 teaspoon water
2 tablespoons soya or goat's milk
approximately ¼ cup wheatgerm
cold pressed oil, for frying

Mix fish with potato, onion, parsley, basil and a little salt.

Beat egg with water. Add half to mixture; mix the other half with the milk.

Shape rissoles. (A ¼ cup flat measuring cup dipped in cold water, then filled with mixture makes nice shapes.) Dip rissoles in egg and milk mixture, then roll through wheatgerm and fry both sides on hot oil showing slight vapour.

Marinaded Grilled Fish

4 fish fillets

Marinade
2 cloves garlic, crushed
2 cm piece green ginger, finely grated
2 tablespoons Maggi seasoning to taste
1 tablespoon lemon juice
½ cup fish or chicken stock

Combine all marinade ingredients and soak fillets in marinade for at least ½ hour.

Place fillets on grill plate and baste with remainder of marinade while cooking.

Oven Baked Fish Cakes

1 egg
2 cups flaked fish (could be leftovers)
1 cup cooked rice
1 onion, finely chopped
3 tablespoons cold pressed oil
squeeze of lemon juice
vegetable salt, if necessary
1 cup finely ground nuts or
    sunflower kernels

Beat egg and add all ingredients, except the nuts. Mix thoroughly. Shape into patties (best to use a ¼ cup flat measuring cup rinsed in cold water). Roll through nuts and place on oiled baking sheet. Bake in 180°C oven until brown, about 20 minutes. Serve hot, garnished with sprigs of parsley.

Oven Baked Bream

4 medium fillets of bream
generous pinch cayenne pepper
2 teaspoons basil
1 teaspoon thyme
lemon juice
¼ cup goat's milk
2 Vita Brits or approximately ¼ cup
    wheatgerm or sesame seeds
1 tablespoon cold pressed oil

Grease small casserole dish; put in 2 fillets. Spread with half the cayenne pepper, then half the herbs. Repeat procedure with another layer of 2 fillets. Then sprinkle with lemon juice and milk. Put crushed Vita Brits, wheatgerm or sesame seeds on top. Sprinkle the cold pressed oil over it and bake in 180°C oven for 30 minutes.

Salmon or Tuna Pie

1 large tin salmon or tuna, drained and
  flaked
1 cup cooked rice
1–2 tomatoes (unsprayed if possible),
  chopped
2 tablespoons finely chopped continental
  parsley
1 egg (optional)
1 teaspoon dried basil
pinch cayenne pepper
pinch vegetable salt, if necessary
approximately ¼ cup wheatgerm or sesame
  seeds
1 tablespoon cold pressed oil

Mix all ingredients, except wheatgerm and oil thoroughly. Put
into greased casserole dish. Cover top with wheatgerm or
sesame seeds and sprinkle with cold pressed oil. Bake in 180°C
oven for 30 minutes.

Salmon Souffle

2 tablespoons goat's or soya milk
2 tablespoons cold pressed oil
1 cup hot mashed potatoes
2 eggs
1 cup mashed salmon
1 tablespoon finely chopped parsley
vegetable salt, if necessary
1 teaspoon dried basil
pinch cayenne pepper
squeeze of lemon juice

Warm milk and oil and thoroughly mix potatoes into liquids while heating. Separate eggs and beat yolks into potato mixture. Stir in fish, parsley, salt, basil, cayenne pepper and lemon juice. Beat egg whites stiffly and fold lightly into mixture. Pour into well greased casserole and bake in 200°C oven until risen and golden brown.

Sprinkle parsley on top.

PROTEIN DISHES

How to make Soya Cream
Soak 1 cup of soya beans for 24 hours in cold water. Bring soya beans to the boil in saucepan while covered with water. Boil 30 minutes. Place boiling hot beans in electric blender, making sure that about 2 cups of bean water or boiling water are present with the beans. Add 3 tablespoons of vegetable oil and a little lemon juice. If necessary, put cloth over blender to prevent hot liquid from spurting out. Turn control off and on to take up the heat. Blend for a few minutes until mixture is very fine and thick. Pour into paper cups and freeze until used.

Note on cooking beans
Beans should be soaked 24 hours prior to cooking them. Soya beans take about 7 hours to cook, or can be cooked overnight in the crockpot on hot for 10 hours. Other beans take between 2–3 hours to cook, or about 4 hours in the crockpot.

Savoury Roast

1 cup Soya Cream or mashed cooked
   soya beans
½ cup corn (optional)
½ cup chopped celery
1 medium-sized onion, chopped
1¼ cups cooked rice
½ cup chopped parsley
Maggi seasoning to taste
½ teaspoon salt (optional)
1 egg
¼ teaspoon mixed herbs or bouquet garni
approximately ¼ cup sesame seeds
1 teaspoon paprika

Mix all ingredients, except last two, spoon into greased casserole
dish and sprinkle with sesame seeds and paprika. Bake for 45
minutes until golden brown.

Soya Cream Rice Loaf

2 eggs (1 hard boiled, 1 beaten)
1 large onion
½ cup celery
1 cup Soya Cream (see page 81)
1 teaspoon cold pressed oil
1 cup wheatgerm
1 small tomato (unsprayed if possible)
1 cup rice
1 stick kombu (chopped and soaked)
Maggi seasoning to taste
vegetable salt to taste

Finely dice all ingredients and put into a greased casserole dish.
Bake for 20–30 minutes in oven at 180ºC.

Vegetable Pie

2 cups cooked haricot beans
1 onion, thinly sliced
1 turnip, grated
1 carrot, grated
1 stick celery, thinly sliced
1 egg, beaten, or 1 rounded teaspoon Orgran
    egg replacer and 2 tablespoons water
Maggi seasoning to taste
¼ cup cubed Savoury Roast (see page 82) or
    TVP, beef flavouring (soaked in hot water
    for 15 minutes)
vegetable salt to taste
1 teaspoon dried basil

Mix beans with TVP or Savoury Roast, onion, turnip, celery
and carrot with a small amount of vegetable stock or water. Add
egg or egg replacer and seasonings and put into a greased
casserole dish and cover with wheatgerm or sesame seeds and
dobs of butter. Bake at 180ºC for 20–30 minutes.

Vegetarian Loaf

2 cups cooked red beans
4 tablespoons cold pressed oil
1 green pepper, finely chopped
½ cup goat's or soya milk
1 cup finely chopped walnuts
½ teaspoon celery seeds
2 cups cooked rice
Maggi seasoning to taste
2 eggs, lightly beaten or 2 rounded
    teaspoons Orgran egg replacer and
    2 tablespoons water

Combine all ingredients and mix well. Turn onto a lightly oiled shallow baking pan and pat into a loaf. Bake in preheated 175°C oven for 30 minutes.

Saluggia Bean Stew

1 cup saluggia beans or brown beans
1 large onion
1 capsicum
1–2 eggs, beaten or 1 rounded teaspoon
    Orgran egg replacer and 2 tablespoons
    water
pinch cayenne pepper
2 cloves
1 small bay leaf
vegetable salt to taste
cold pressed oil, for frying

Soak beans for 24 hours then cook until soft. Chop onion and capsicum, then sauté onion in oil until onion is transparent, about 5 minutes. Add bay leaf and cloves. Simmer for about 10 minutes, then add beans, egg, cayenne pepper and salt. Cook for another 5 minutes.

Barlotti or Kidney Bean Loaf

2 cups kidney or barlotti beans
1 bay leaf
3 cloves
1 tablespoon cold pressed oil
1 onion, finely chopped
¾ cup carrots, grated
¾ cup parsnips, grated
1 egg, beaten
1 level teaspoon Maggi seasoning
vegetable salt (optional)

Cook beans with bay leaf and cloves until soft. Drain, add oil
and other ingredients, combine well and cook in casserole dish
in oven at 180ºC.

Opposite: Stephen's Carob Cake (page 120)
Overleaf: Oven Baked Bream (page 77)

Kidney Bean or Brown Bean Croquettes

1 cup kidney beans or brown beans
3 medium-sized cooked potatoes, mashed
1 onion, chopped finely
pinch cayenne pepper
1 teaspoon Maggi seasoning
vegetable salt to taste
1 egg
1–1½ cups wheatgerm
cold pressed oil, for frying
parsley sprigs, for serving

Cook beans until soft and drain in colander. Vitamise or mash with a fork until fine. Mix beans with mashed potatoes. Sauté onion in oil until browned, then add to mixture together with cayenne pepper, Maggi seasoning and salt. Mix thoroughly. Form either round or sausage-like rolls.

Beat egg with a little water. Roll croquettes first through wheatgerm, then through beaten egg and through the wheatgerm again. Fry in deep oil until brown and crisp. Drain on greaseproof paper. Serve with parsley.

Cannelini Bean Croquettes

1 cup cannelini beans
1–2 onions
3 medium-sized cooked potatoes
¼ cup chopped parsley
1 teaspoon Maggi seasoning
½ teaspoon tumeric
½ teaspoon paprika
cayenne pepper, as required
vegetable salt to taste
1 egg
1 teaspoon goat's milk
1–1½ cups wheatgerm
cold pressed oil, for frying
parsley sprigs, for serving

Cook the beans until soft. Chop onions and sauté until slightly browned. Mash beans and potatoes and mix with onions, parsley, Maggi seasoning, tumeric, paprika, cayenne pepper and salt. Knead and make into balls. Slightly flatten balls. Beat egg together with the milk. Put the croquettes through this first and then through the wheatgerm. Fry in hot oil until brown on each side. Serve with parsley.

Chick Pea Casserole

1 cup chick peas
1 cup spinach, chopped
1 onion
1 tablespoon cold pressed oil
1 clove garlic, finely crushed
¼ cup chopped red capsicum
1 tomato (unsprayed if possible), chopped
½ teaspoon ground ginger
2 cloves
1 egg, beaten
2 tablespoons barley flour
Maggi seasoning to taste
1 teaspoon vegetable salt

Soak chick peas in water for 24 hours, then cook until soft.
Chop onion. Heat oil in frying pan. Sauté onion, garlic and
capsicum for a few minutes. Then add spinach and tomato and
simmer for a few minutes with ginger and cloves. Add all other
ingredients and mix together. Put in oiled casserole dish. Bake
in 180ºC oven for 20–30 minutes.

Lima and Green Bean Dish

2 eggs or 2 rounded teaspoons Orgran egg
  replacer and 4 tablespoons water
½ cup chopped shallots
1 cup cooked lima beans
1 cup slightly cooked green beans
½ cup corn (optional)
2 tablespoons chopped nuts
¼ cup TVP, beef flavouring (soaked in hot
  water for 15 minutes)
2 tablespoons maize meal or barley flour
¼ cup wheatgerm
little cold pressed oil

Beat eggs or prepare egg replacer, then add shallots and cooked
beans. Add all other ingredients and put in oiled casserole dish.
Top with wheatgerm and sprinkle a little cold pressed oil on
top. Cook in 175–200ºC oven for 20 minutes.

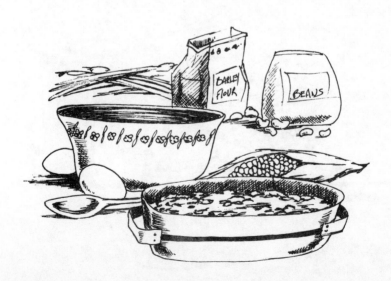

Lentil or Split Pea Patties

1 cup lentils or split peas
¼ cup TVP mince (optional)
1 egg
¼ teaspoon thyme
½ teaspoon tumeric
½ teaspoon vegetable salt
1 small onion, very finely chopped
rolled oats or rolled barley
cold pressed oil, for frying

Just cover lentils with water and cook until soft, about 15 minutes. Just cover TVP in boiling water for 10 minutes. Beat egg in bowl and add thyme, tumeric and salt, then onion, lentils and TVP. Stir thoroughly and add sufficient rolled oats to make a fairly solid consistency. Heat oil in frying pan (just enough oil to cover frying pan bottom). Take tablespoonsful of mixture and form patties while putting them in the pan. Flatten them slightly with a fork when in the pan. Fry until golden brown on both sides.

Lentil Roast

1 cup brown lentils
1 egg
1 onion, grated or finely chopped
2 tablespoons chopped parsley
1 medium-sized carrot, grated
pinch thyme
1 cup goat's milk
¼ cup tahini
1 teaspoon vegetable salt (optional)
½ cup rolled oats or rice
approximately ¼ cup sesame seeds

Cook lentils until soft, about 20 minutes. Break egg into bowl and mix with onion, parsley, carrot, thyme, milk, tahini and salt. Mix well, then add lentils and rolled oats. Pour mixture into greased casserole dish, sprinkle whole sesame seeds on top and bake in 175°C oven for 30–45 minutes.

Split Pea Roast

2 cups split peas
3 cups water
½ cup crumbled tofu
½ cup leftover vegetable loaf or other loaf
1 medium-sized carrot, grated
1 large onion, grated
1 cup chopped leeks
1 teaspoon dried basil
pinch cayenne
little vegetable salt
1 egg, beaten
1 teaspoon Maggi seasoning

Soak split peas overnight in water, then cook until soft. Mix together thoroughly with other ingredients. Bake in 175°C oven until set. Serve hot with mint sauce and vegetables, cold on salad, or as a sandwich filling.

Mung Beans

1 cup mung beans
¾ litre (1¼ pints) water
Maggi seasoning to taste
3 teaspoons cold pressed oil
1 onion, finely sliced
1 cup cubed Savoury Roast (see page 82) or
    ¼ cup TVP, beef flavouring (soaked in hot
    water for 15 minutes)
1 stick kombu (if available), chopped and
    soaked
1 teaspoon tumericc
1 teaspoon ground coriander

Soak mung beans overnight. Add Maggi seasoning to soaking water, then cook until beans are just tender. Do not overcook. Heat oil and gently sauté onions and Savoury Roast, if using, until onions transparent. Add to mung beans, retaining cooking liquid. If using TVP, and kombu, add to mixture along with tumeric and coriander. Simmer without overcooking beans. Add vegetable salt if necessary. Serve rice as an accompaniment.

Sunflower Seed Loaf

1½ cups ground sunflower seeds
¾ cup finely ground sesame seed meal
½ cup chopped walnuts
1 cup cooked lentils
½ cup grated raw beetroot
3 tablespoons minced chives or shallots
2 eggs, beaten slightly, or 2 rounded
   teaspoons Orgran egg replacer and
   4 tablespoons water
2 tablespoons lemon juice
½ cup diced celery
½ cup cooked buckwheat or brown rice
Maggi seasoning to taste
1 tablespoon cold pressed oil

Blend together all ingredients, and press into an oiled baking dish. Bake at 170ºC until done, about 60 minutes. Serve hot from the oven with a raw salad.

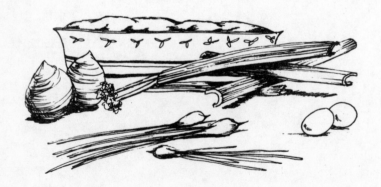

Savoury Nut Casserole

3 small eggs beaten with
  1 tablespoon goat's milk or soya milk
2 heaped tablespoons finely chopped
  walnuts
2 medium-sized onions, finely chopped
1 tablespoon finely chopped parsley or
  celery leaves
1 cup rolled oats
1 cup cubed marinated tofu
1–2 teaspoons dried sweet basil
pinch mixed herbs
vegetable salt to taste
approximately ¼ cup sesame seeds

Mix all ingredients except sesame seeds together and place in a greased casserole dish. Top with sesame seeds. Bake in moderate oven (180°C) for 30-45 minutes.

Nut Galatine

1 carrot
1 medium-sized onion
1 cup chopped mixed nuts
1 cup brown rice
2 tablespoons chopped parsley
1 tablespoon cold pressed oil
1 large egg, beaten, or 1 rounded teaspoon
  Orgran egg replacer and 2 tablespoons
  water

Grate carrot and chop onion, then mix together with nuts, rice and parsley. Add oil and bind with beaten egg or egg replacer. Press mixture into a well greased savoury roll jar and steam for about 2½ hours.

VEGETABLES

Vegetables should **not be peeled**, but **scrubbed only**. By grating, dicing or slicing vegetables, such as carrots, beetroot, pumpkin, they cook much quicker and not so many valuable elements are lost.

The best ways to cook vegetables are baking in the oven, or the waterless way. The best utensils to use for cooking are stainless steel, enamel, Corning Ware, Pyrex and other ovenware. **Never** use aluminium cooking utensils. The aluminium is a poison which is absorbed by the food. It has a bad effect on the stomach and bowels, and deposits in the brain can cause Alzheimer's disease.

Cooking vegetables at boiling temperature destroys both vitamins and enzymes, which are essential for proper digestion of your food. Cooking below boiling temperature as in waterless cooking and crock pots, retains the vitamins and other valuable nutrients. Waterless cooking is by far the best method. To be able to do this a stainless steel saucepan specially equipped for this way of cooking is required. Some even have a thermometer fitted into the lid with a red mark warning when the temperature is too high.

The procedure for waterless cooking is as follows: Just cover the bottom of the saucepan with water, and add a little oil. Place the clean vegetables in the saucepan on medium to high heat. When enough vapour appears to make the lid ride on the vapour, reduce the heat as low as possible (a flame distributor can be placed in between). Turn the lid so that it continues to ride on the vapour. If lid lifts up, temperature is still a little too high. Leave vegetables on this low temperature for the required cooking time. If you have a gas stove, a little more water may need to be added.

Do not add salt or soda to any fresh vegetables when cooking them. With the 'waterless cooking' method all natural salts, minerals and vitamins, as well as the flavour of the food, are retained.

To finish off and to add to the flavour a little modified butter (see product information) or soft butter can be added before serving or with some vegetables a little yoghurt. Also herbs or harmless spices can be added.

Approximate cooking times

beans, string, wax, fresh lima	15-20 minutes
beetroot, sliced; onions, whole	20-25 minutes
beetroot, grated; carrots, grated	10-15 minutes
broccoli; cauliflower; celery; kale	8-10 minutes
carrots, whole; small turnips; pumpkin with skin	20-25 minutes
corn; brussel sprouts	10-12 minutes
eggplant; leeks; capsicum; squash	8-10 minutes
greens; cabbage; tomatoes	3-5 minutes
onions, sliced; fresh peas	5-8 minutes
parsnips, sliced	10-15 minutes
potatoes, sweet, halves	25-30 minutes
potatoes, small or halves	30-35 minutes

Carrots

Scrub carrots, cut into slice or fingers 5 cm (2") long. Waterless cook with a teaspoon of cold pressed safflower or sunflower oil until cooked. Top with finely chopped parsley.

Parsnips

Cook in the same way as carrots.

Green Beans

Take threads off beans, break in two or three pieces. Wash beans and waterless cook. Top with a little nutmeg.

Peas

Shell peas and waterless cook. Top with chopped parsley or mint.

Snow Peas or Sugar Snap Peas

Do not shell. Thread peas and waterless cook. No need for any topping. Can be served with a little butter when on low allergy diet.

Baby Carrots and Sugar Snap Peas

Wash and scrub carrots and waterless cook with a little modified butter. Add the threaded sugar peas when carrots are half cooked. Top with finely chopped parsley when serving.

Pumpkin

Cut pumpkin in cubes, skin included, and waterless cook. Top with chopped parsley or watercress. If cooked in oven, cut in large pieces or even bake the whole pumpkin. Oil baking dish with cold pressed oil.

Beetroot

Wash and scrub beets. Cut into thin slices or coarsely grate. Waterless cook.

Fry one finely chopped onion in cold pressed safflower oil until transparent. Add to cooked beetroot. Also add a little lemon juice.

Use arrowroot if needs thickening.

Swedes

Wash and scrub the skin. Waterless cook. After swedes are soft simmer in sauce (for recipe, see cauliflower sauce recipe on page 101. Dust with a little nutmeg when serving.

Sweetcorn

Simmer in 2 cm water for about 15 minutes.
   Serve with yoghurt or light sour cream.

Spinach

Wash and chop spinach and waterless cook.
   Mix with a little yoghurt or light sour cream.

Endive

Prepare in the same way as spinach. Add some grated Granny Smith apple.

Cauliflower

Divide cauliflower into even pieces. Take off hard stalks. Put in vegetable salt and water for about 15 minutes. Then place in saucepan with stalks down and waterless cook.

Make a sauce using ½ cup goat's milk, 1 tablespoon rice flour and 1 teaspoon cummin seed or chopped parsley. Add flour to cold milk and bring to the boil while stirring with French whisk. Reduce heat and add cummin or parsley, continuing to stir until thickened.

Pour over cauliflower when serving. Dust with nutmeg, if required, but only if no cummin seed is used.

Broccoli

Divide broccoli in pieces. Take off hard stalks. Waterless cook and serve with a little modified butter.

White or Savoy Cabbage

Clean and shred cabbage. Waterless cook with a little cold pressed oil and caraway seeds (to avoid flatulence).

Brussels Sprouts

Cook in the same way as white cabbage.

Red Cabbage with Granny Smith Apples

Wash and core one large Granny Smith apple. Cut into small pieces and waterless cook. Wash and shred the cabbage. Add to cooked apples with 1 bay leaf and 2 cloves.

When both apples and cabbage are soft, mix thoroughly. Thicken fluid with arrowroot. A little lemon juice can also be added.

Leek or Onions

Remove any dry, dirty leaves. Cut leeks into 2 cm (¾") pieces, including green parts. Wash very thoroughly in a lot of water. Strain, then place in saucepan and waterless cook. Onions should be cooked in the same way, using either very small onions or onion quarters with larger onions. Add a little lemon juice when cooked.

Make a sauce from ½ cup goat's milk and 1 tablespoon rice flour using method described for cauliflower sauce on page 101. Add to leeks and simmer for a few minutes.

Jerusalem Artichokes

Wash and shrub artichokes, taking out any bad parts. Cut into 4 cm (1½") pieces. Waterless cook. Simmer in sauce the same as that prepared for leeks.

Vegetable Mould

1 cup diced mixed vegetables such as:
   carrot or pumpkin or beetroot or parsley
   and beans or peas
   and zucchini or choko or squash
   and shallots or onions
½ cup of water
½ cup of vegetable juice
1 rounded teaspoon agar agar

Waterless cook vegetables until just tender.

Heat water until at boiling point, add juice, then bring to boil again. Stir in agar for one minute. Pour a little into mould rinsed with cold water. Add vegetables and pour in remaining agar mixture. Mix vegetables and agar mixture with spoon, leave to cool, then put in fridge and turn out of mould onto a plate.

Beetroot Mould

3 cups cubed cooked beetroot
2 cups water, including juice of beetroot
3 rounded teaspoons agar agar
juice of 1 lemon

Heat water and juice to boiling point, add agar agar and lemon juice, stir and take off heat. Rinse mould with cold water, put some agar mixture in mould, add the beetroot then fill up with agar mixture.

Cool and put out of mould onto plate.

Note: If prefered, use individual moulds for each person rather than one large mould.

Stir Fried Vegetable Dish

2 tablespoons cold pressed oil
1 cup sliced onions
1 cup sliced beans
1 cup sliced carrots
1 cup sliced celery
1 clove garlic, crushed and chopped
a little Maggi seasoning
1 cup water
2 teaspoons arrowroot blended
  in a little water

Heat oil in heavy frying pan. Put in all vegetables, adding celery
last. Stir for a few minutes, then add Maggi seasoning and water.
Cover and simmer for 5 minutes, then add arrowroot while
stirring. Serve at once.

Ratatouille

2 large onions
2 capsicums (1 red, 1 green)
1 eggplant
4 zucchini
3 ripe tomatoes (unsprayed if possible),
    peeled
1 tablespoon chopped fresh basil
1 tablespoon chopped fresh oregano
pinch cayenne pepper
2 tablespoons chopped fresh parsley
1–2 tablespoons cold pressed oil

Cut vegetables in slices or bite-size pieces. Heat oil and saute
onion until transparent, add capsicum, eggplant, zucchini and
tomatoes. Simmer for 30 minutes or desired time. Add herbs.

STAPLE DISHES

By staple dishes we mean such foods as potatoes, rice, buckwheat and pasta, even whole millet can be used as such.

Potatoes can be cooked in a saucepan or baked in their jackets. Before cooking, scrub with a brush and take out any bad spots. Green potatoes must not be used. When cooked in a saucepan, pour off any water left after potatoes are soft and put back on element for a few minutes until potatoes are dry and floury. If potatoes are baked, they take about an hour in a moderate oven.

A variety of recipes for preparing potatoes are provided in this section. Alternatively rice can be eaten, either as is or using the recipes provided.

Potato Hotpot with Lettuce

4 medium potatoes
1 onion
1 tablespoon cold pressed oil
¼ cup goat's milk
a little vegetable salt
1 cup cooked haricot beans (see note
    page 81)
2 cups shredded lettuce leaves

Cook potatoes in about ½ cup water. Chop onion and fry in oil. Add to potatoes and mash together, adding milk, salt and beans. Lastly add shredded lettuce leaves.

Hutspot

4 medium potatoes
1 cup diced carrots
1 large onion
1 tablespoon cold pressed oil
¼ cup goat's milk
Maggi seasoning to taste
vegetable salt, if required

Cook potatoes and carrots together in about ½ cup water. Chop onion and fry in oil. Add to potatoes and mash together with the milk, Maggi seasoning and salt.

Serve as it is or put in a casserole dish, make lines with a fork and brown for about 10 minutes in the oven.

Potato Casserole

1 onion, chopped
2 tablespoons cold pressed oil
1 teaspoon tumeric
½ teaspoon sweet basil
½ teaspoon chervil
¼ teaspoon coriander
½ cup finely chopped celery or chives
  and parsley mixed
½ teaspoon vegetable salt
2 tablespoons rice flour
2 cups water mixed with Maggi seasoning
3 cups diced cooked potatoes

Sauté onion in oil until beginning to brown. Add tumeric, sweet basil, chervil, coriander, celery or chives and parsley, salt, and stir well. Add rice flour and water mixed with Maggi seasoning. Stir until thickened. Add potatoes, then place mixture in casserole dish.

Bake in oven at 180°C for 20–30 minutes.

Spiced Potatoes

2 tablespoons cold pressed oil
1 tomato (unsprayed if possible),
   finely chopped
4 tablespoons green pepper, diced
¼ teaspoon cayenne pepper
¼ teaspoon ground tumeric
¼ teaspoon ground allspice
¼ teaspoon ground ginger
¼ teaspoon vegetable salt
½ teaspoon ground coriander
5 large cooked potatoes, diced

Heat oil in a large heavy frying pan over a moderate heat. Add tomato, green pepper, cayenne pepper, tumeric, allspice, ginger, salt and coriander. Cook, stirring constantly, for 2 minutes. Add potatoes and cook, stirring until potatoes are coated with spices and heated through.

Potato Pancakes

4 large potatoes, grated
2 eggs or 1 rounded teaspoon Orgran egg
   replacer and 2 tablespoons water
½ cup cornmeal or buckwheat flour
vegetable salt to taste
pinch cayenne pepper
2 tablespoons parsley, finely chopped
1 teaspoon dried basil
cold pressed oil, for frying

Put raw grated potatoes into a basin, then mix two unbeaten eggs or egg replacer, cornmeal or flour, salt, pepper, parsley and basil into the potatoes.

When thoroughly mixed, drop tablespoonsful of mixture into a pan with very hot oil and fry until a light brown on both sides.

Fried Rice

1–2 tablespoons cold pressed oil
medium–large sized onion, chopped
3–4 cups cold cooked brown rice or barley
    (soaked in water overnight before
    cooking)
½–⅔ cup diced carrot, half cooked
¼–½ cup diced red capsicum or chopped
    celery
1 cup peas
a little vegetable salt
1 tablespoon Maggi seasoning
1 cup chopped shallots

Heat oil, sauté onion for a few minutes, and then add rice. Break up lumps and stir to distribute oil evenly. Sauté a little longer to crisp the rice. Add vegetables and salt.

When uniformly heated add Maggi seasoning. Add shallots.

Optional ingredients
½ cup of any of the following: chopped water chestnuts, bamboo shoots, pineapple pieces, soya beans or chick peas, chopped up softly scrambled egg.

Rice and Curry Dish

2 cups brown rice or barley
    (soaked in water overnight)
3 cups water
1 teaspoon cold pressed oil
1 tablespoon dried basil
vegetable salt to taste
1 large onion, chopped
1½ cups chopped celery
½ cup chopped choko
½ cup green bean pieces
1 tomato, (unsprayed if possible) chopped
2 cups Savoury Roast (see recipe page 82)
    or ½ cup TVP, beef flavouring (soaked in
    hot water for 15 minutes)
2 teaspoons health curry
3 tablespoons yoghurt

Bring rice to boil in water with oil. Simmer for about 1 hour.
Add basil and a little vegetable salt.

Curry mixture
Fry onion in a little cold pressed oil and add vegetables and
Savoury Roast or TVP, then curry. Lastly add yoghurt.

Buckwheat Roast

1 cup buckwheat
1 large onion, chopped
1 tablespoon cold pressed oil
½ cup diced capsicum (optional)
1 cup diced celery
1 egg, beaten, or 1 rounded tablespoon
   Orgran egg replacer and 2 tablespoons
   water
Maggi seasoning to taste

Boil buckwheat in water until cooked, for about 10 minutes. Sauté onion in oil until slightly brown, then add capsicum and celery. Mix together with cooked buckwheat. Stir in beaten egg or egg replacer and Maggi seasoning if required. Put in oiled casserole dish and bake in oven at 180ºC for about 15 minutes.

Note: Onion, celery and capsicum can be cooked together with buckwheat rather than frying. This is a better way for people with liver or gallbladder trouble.

Barley and Spinach Pasta

250 g (9 oz) barley and spinach pasta
2 cups water
1 tablespoon cold pressed oil
1 onion, chopped
2 cloves garlic, crushed
2 tomatoes (unsprayed if possible), chopped
Maggi seasoning to taste
3 tablespoons yoghurt or light sour cream

Bring water to boil first, then add pasta and cook for about
5 minutes. Drain. Heat oil and sauté onions and garlic until
soft, then add tomatoes and Maggi seasoning. Before serving
stir yoghurt or sour cream through pasta.

Bani Goreng (Vegetarian Indonesian Dish)

250 g (9 oz) spinach vermicelli
5 shallots bulbs or spring onions
3 garlic cloves, crushed
1 tablespoon cold pressed oil
1 cup diced celery
1 cup shredded cabbage
1 cup green beans, sliced
2 cups chopped leeks or spring onion tips
1 cup Savoury Roast (see page 82) or
    similar to commercial product
1 teaspoon ginger powder
Maggi seasoning to taste
juice of 1 lemon
vegetable salt to taste
2 eggs (optional)
1 tablespoon water (optional)
60-80 g (3 oz) olives

Boil vermicelli in a lot of water until cooked. Separate and drain in colander. Chop shallots or spring onions and sauté with garlic in oil until slightly browned. Add celery, cabbage, beans, leeks and spring onion tips and sauté another 10 minutes. Add Soyabean Roast and ginger powder. Leave for a few more minutes on low heat. Stir this mixture through the cooked vermicelli together with Maggi seasoning and lemon juice. Simmer for about 10 minutes. Add salt.

Make omelette by beating eggs, then adding water and beating until frothy. Fry omelette on both sides until slightly brown, then cut into strips.

Put Bani Goreng into serving dish and decorate with strips of omelette and olives.

Savoury Millet

1¼ cups hulled millet
3 cups water
1 tablespoon grapeseed oil
1 large onion
1 cup chopped celery
1 cup peas
1 tomato, cubed
Maggi seasoning to taste
cold pressed oil, for frying

Cook millet in water with the oil until soft. Chop onion and sauté with celery until onion transparent. Add to millet together with peas, tomato and Maggi seasoning. Can be pressed into cakes and fried on both sides in a little oil.

GRAINS AND DESSERTS

None of the recipes used contain wheat as this is one of the foods to which people are most allergic. For those who do not know, buckwheat is not wheat.

If you are allergic to any of the other grains these can usually be substituted with one to which you are not allergic.

There is a non-allergy baking powder available at health food stores. The desserts contain some artificial sweetening. Be sure to buy the most natural type.

Important note
Orgran egg replacer can be used in place of eggs: 1 heaped teaspoon of egg replacer mixed with 2 tablespoons of water is equivalent to one egg.

Waffles

Cashew-Oat
2¼ cups water
½ cup wholemeal flour
1 cup rolled oats
½ cup raw cashews
1 tablespoon cold pressed oil
pinch vegetable salt (optional)

Multi-Grain
2¼ cups water
½ cup rye flour
½ cup wholemeal flour
½ cup soya flour
½ cup rolled oats
pinch 1 tablespoon cold pressed oil
pinch vegetable salt (optional)

Buckwheat-Oat
2¼ cups water
½ cup buckwheat flour
¼ cup soya flour
1½ cups rolled oats
1 tablespoon cold pressed oil
pinch vegetable salt (optional)

Combine all ingredients in electric blender until light and foamy. Let stand while waffle iron is heating. When red light turns off, put about ½ cup of mixture in waffle iron. (If not enough or too much, adjust with next waffle.) Do not open iron until waffle is cooked, about 8–10 minutes, when little or no steam escapes.

If waffle is too thick and not crunchy add a little more water to mixture. Keep warm in low oven if necessary.

Serve with tahini.

Yeast-free Pancakes

2 eggs, beaten
1 cup buckwheat flour
½ litre (2 cups) goat's milk
2 tablespoons cold pressed oil
  (more if required)
little vegetable salt if necessary

Mix eggs into the flour and salt, gradually adding milk and
1 tablespoon oil.
  Heat 1 tablespoon oil in frying pan and make thin pancakes.
Slightly brown on each side.
  Serve with tahini or fill with Savoury Filling and roll up.

Savoury Filling
1 tablespoon cold pressed oil
1 medium-sized onion, finely chopped
2 tablespoons rice flour
pinch vegetable salt
½ teaspoon sweet basil
1 cup well-cooked brown lentils
1 tablespoon chopped parsley

Heat oil in pan and cook onion. Stir in flour, salt and basil.
Let mixture bubble. Gradually add milk, stirring all the time.
  Take from heat, then add parsley.

Pikelets

½ cup fine millet flour
½ cup fine barley flour
½ cup soya flour
1 tablespoon fine cornmeal
1 tablespoon ground linseed
1 tablespoon sunflower kernels
  or ground nuts
½ teaspoon cinnamon
300 ml (½ pint) water
2 teaspoons Orgran egg replacer and
  4 tablespoons water
pinch vegetable salt
herbs to taste, if required
cold pressed oil, for frying

Mix ingredients and beat with electric beater if possible or use a whisk. Oil frying pan and heat until a light vapour appears. Drop in tablespoonsful of mixture. Cover pan with lid. Fry both sides of pikelets until slightly browned, keeping lid on all the time at a medium temperature.

Serve when ready or put in containers lined with greaseproof paper. Put paper between layers to avoid pikelets sticking together.

Cornmeal Pancakes

1½ cups fine yellow cornmeal (maize)
½ teaspoon vegetable salt
2 cups goat's or soya milk
2 tablespoons cold pressed oil
1 egg yolk, slightly beaten
1 egg white, stiffly beaten

Stir together dry ingredients. Add milk, 1 tablespoon of oil, egg yolk, and fold in egg white.

   Drop spoonfuls of mixture into hot oiled pan, and cook until golden brown on both sides.

Corn Bread Cakes

1 cup unrefined yellow cornmeal
1½ cups boiling water
½ teaspoon vegetable salt
2 tablespoons cold pressed oil

Add cornmeal all at once to salted boiling water. Stir until it clings together in a ball, pulling away from the sides of the saucepan. Remove from the heat. Add oil and beat briskly.

   Place spoonfuls of mixture onto a lightly oiled tray and flatten with a fork. Bake at 200ºC until nicely browned, about 30 minutes.

Stephen's Carob Cake

3 cups fine barley flour, fine rice flour or
   fine cornmeal
2 eggs (see note page 115)
3 teaspoons low allergy baking powder
125 g (4½ oz) soft butter
   (Prefer or Dairy Soft)
100 g (3½ oz) sugarless carob buds
2 tablespoons carob powder
artificial sweetening, equivalent to ¾ cup
   sugar
½ teaspoon vanilla essence
½ cup milk and 1 cup water or 1½ cups
   water

Line bottom of 20 cm (8") baking tin with greaseproof paper,
then grease sides of tin and paper.

Sift flour and mix in the baking powder. Cream soft butter
with sweetener until fluffy. Add 1 egg first, or half the egg
replacer, then beat well with electric beater or Bamix. Melt
carob buds in small bowl above boiling water.

Mix milk and water, add half of this together with the melted
carob buds to mixture, then beat again. Add half the flour,
the carob powder and vanilla essence while beating. Now add
the other egg or remaining egg replacer, then the remaining
milk and beat together with the remaining flour. Beat
thoroughly and pour into the greased baking tin. Bake in 150ºC
oven for 50 minutes. Cool on rack. When cold cover with
Tofu Cream, and decorate with almonds, hazelnuts or other
nuts and pepitas.

Tofu Cream
300 g (10½ oz) tofu, drained
1 tablespoon water
1–2 tablespoons honey or equivalent
   amount of sweetener
1 teaspoon vanilla essence

Blend and whip all ingredients till creamy. Vanilla essence can be replaced with 1 teaspoon of almond essence or 1 tablespoon of coconut cream, depending on your allergies.

Pumpkin Pie

Pastry
150 g (5 ¼ oz) butter
1½ cups rice flour
½ cup arrowroot
1 teaspoon lemon juice

Work butter into flour and arrowroot with two knives, add lemon juice and mix into ingredients. Line pie plate with pastry, moulding with hand.

Filling
500 g (1 lb) pumpkin
½ teaspoon each nutmeg, cinnamon and
    ginger
¼ teaspoon all spice
2 eggs (see note page 115)
artificial sweetener equivalent to ¼ cup
    sugar
1 cup soya milk
3 tablespoons soya milk powder

Cook pumpkin, then add spices, eggs, sweetener and milks. Mix in blender until creamy.

Place in pie shell, and cook at 200ºC for 10 minutes, then at 180ºC for 35 minutes.

Milk Porridge

4 cups goat's milk or soya milk or
  2 cups goat's milk and 2 cups water
4 rounded tablespoons millet meal
1 rounded tablespoon cornmeal
1 rounded tablespoon rice flour
2 rounded tablespoons rolled oats
  or rolled barley
1 rounded tablespoon soya flour (optional)

Combine all ingredients in a saucepan. Bring to nearly boiling, stirring constantly. Turn to a low heat and continue stirring for another ½ minute. Leave simmering with lid on until cooked.

If the porridge is too thick add more milk or water.

Custard

2 cups goat's milk
1½ tablespoons (level) rice or barley flour
½ tablespoon arrowroot
2 eggs
2 teaspoons pure vanilla
artificial sweetener equivalent to
  1 tablespoon sugar

Mix all ingredients together, stirring with French whisk until thickened. Serve hot or cold.

Note: Do not replace eggs with Orgran egg replacer in this recipe.

Carob Pudding (cold)

2 cups goat's milk
4 tablespoons rice flour
1 tablespoon arrowroot
4 tablespoons carob powder
artificial sweetener equivalent to
   2 tablespoons sugar

Mix ingredients and bring to boil while stirring with French whisk. Boil a few minutes while thickening. Rinse mould with cold water, then pour mixture into mould. Serve with cold custard (see page 122) or coconut cream.

Sesame Crackers

¼ cup melted butter, or oil
1 cup cold water
1 teaspoon vegetable salt (optional)
¾ cup sesame seeds (crushed in blender)
1 cup fine maize or buckwheat flour
1 cup fine millet flour
1 cup fine rice flour
¼ cup whole sesame seed

Emulsify butter, water and salt in blender. Mix into crushed sesame seeds and flour. Roll out or press, very thinly, onto greased tray. Press the whole sesame seeds into the top and cut into squares. Bake in a hot oven for 10-15 minutes. Turn oven down to 130°C and leave until completely cooked and dry, to the extent that they can be shaken of the tray. Cool on rack, covered with greaseproof paper.

Scottish Oatcakes

2 cups fine oatmeal
1 teaspoon vegetable salt
¼ cup cold pressed oil
⅔ cups cold water

Mix all ingredients. Roll out or press onto floured board until as thin as possible (approximately 2 mm/⅛″). Cut into rounds and place on greased tray. Bake in hot oven for 10-15 minutes. Then turn oven down to 130⁰C and leave until completely cooked and dry to the extent they can be shaken off the tray.

Cool on rack covered with greaseproof paper.

Easy Bread

1 cup fine barley flour
1 cup fine buckwheat flour
1 cup fine millet flour
2 eggs (see note page 115)
1½ cups soya milk

Sift flours. Beat eggs, and add to flours. Stir in soya milk, and mix thoroughly. Put in greased loaf tin (24 x 10 cm/10″ x 4″). Bake in 180⁰C oven for approximately 1½ hours.

Sour Dough Bread

Sour Dough (leavening agent)

Mix 1 cup of rye or whole wheat or millet flour with sufficient water to make a stiff dough. Cover and put in a warm place (30°C). Leave for 8 days, when the dough has developed a pleasant aroma. It is now ready to be used in bread making.

Making the Bread

1 piece of sour dough (about the size of a large apple)
700 ml (2¾ cups) warm water, or warm water and buttermilk
7 cups rye flour (or whole wheat or millet)
½ teaspoon vegetable salt
1 tablespoon caraway seed

Place sour dough and liquid in a warm bowl.

Add half the flour and mix thoroughly, then add the remainder of the ingredients and mix well for a few minutes.

Now take out a piece the size of a large apple for the next bread making session. Place the remaining dough in two greased baking tins (size of orange cake tins) or make two oval loaves and put on a floured cooking sheet, also greased. Cover with plasitc bags to protect against draughts. Put in a warm place (30°C) for about 24 hours. (In summer, dough can be placed in the sun during the day.)

Preheat oven to 160-190°C (350-400°F). Place bread in oven for 50-60 minutes. Cool on a rack, wrap in luncheon paper and store in plastic bag in the fridge.

This bread will keep for a long time.

Scones

1 cup barley flour
1 cup rice or buckwheat flour
2 teaspoons low allergy baking powder
1 teaspoon vegetable salt
½ teaspoon cayenne pepper
½ teaspoon celery seed
1 tablespoon grated onion
½ cup cold pressed oil
½ cup goat's or soya milk

Mix dry ingredients, then add herbs, onion, oil and milk. Beat
well with Bamix or electric beater. Divide into twelve scones
and put on sheet. Bake in hot oven for about 10 minutes.

Note
- In place of herbs, ½ cup of mashed pumpkin can be used.
- Scones made from other than wheat flour do not rise as well.

INDEX

WHERE TO GO FOR
FURTHER HELP

The people listed below will direct you to your nearest doctor or naturopath experienced in candidiasis, food sensitivities, allergies etc.

If tests for food sentivities, candida or other common allergy problems prove negative, then chemical intolerance (the Twentieth Century Syndrome) could be the possible cause of your problem. To get assistance in determining whether this is your problem, contact The Institute for Nutritional and Environmental Medicine: (02) 977 7888.

New South Wales

ANTA*
Sydney (02) 267 5285

Australian Holistic Biologics Laboratory†
Sydney (02) 221 5488

Fountaindale Clinic
Central Coast (043) 62 1871
(Run by the authors of this book)

Alex McDonald ND
Moss Vale (048) 87 7225

James and Kerry Harrison ND
Windsor (045) 77 6215

Graham Quilty
Tumut (065) 52 4895

Maurice Finkel M Sc
Kingscliff (Northern NSW) (066) 74 2407

Queensland

Health World Pty Ltd
Brisbane (07) 262 5688

Allergy Association of Australia
(P O Box 45, Woody Point 4019)

Victoria

ANTA*
contact Sydney (02) 267 5285

South Australia

Allergy Association of Australia
(P O Box 104, North Adelaide 5006)

Dr Doug Dickman DC
Adelaide (08) 337 8572

Peter Farnsworth
Naturopath and Herbalist
(Unit 2, 22 Byron Street, Glenelg 5045)
(08) 233 6490

Tasmania

Allergy Recognition and Management Inc.
(P O Box 2, Sandy Bay 7005)

West Australia

ANTA*
contact Sydney (02) 267 5285

Karrinyup Allergy Clinic and Resource Centre
Perth (09) 246 1822

* Australian Natural Therapists Association
   (P O Box 522, Sutherland 2232)
   (02) 521 2063

† They operate the first Australian-based ALCAT food sensitivity
   computer. This is the most advanced and accurate method in the
   world today. They also use the older Cytotoxic method, which,
   with careful procedures, is also very useful and less expensive. It is
   not possible to receive a Medicare rebate for either method.